D1824625

Walking the Sussex Border Path

David Bathurst

Photographs by David Bathurst

S.B. Publications

By the same author:

The Selsey Tram
Six Of The Best
The Jennings Companion
Financial Penalties
Around Chichester In Old Photographs
Here's A Pretty Mess!
Magisterial Lore
The Beaten Track (republished as The Big Walks Of Great Britain, republished again as
The Big Walks Of The North and The Big Walks Of The South)
Poetic Justice
That's My Girl
Walking The Coastline Of Sussex
Best Sussex Walks
Let's Take It From The Top
Walking The Disused Railways Of Sussex
(republished as Walking The Disused Railways Of Sussex And Surrey)
Once More From The Top
Sussex Top Tens
Walking The Kent Coast From End To End
Walking The South Coast Of England
Walking The Riversides Of Sussex
Anyone For Tenors?
Walking The Triangulation Points Of Sussex
Walking The Disused Railways Of Kent

To Lizanne

First published in 2012 by S.B. Publications, 14 Bishopstone Road, Seaford, East Sussex.
Tel: 01323 893498   Email: sbpublications@tiscali.co.uk

ISBN 978-185770-367-2

Designed and Typeset by EH Graphics, East Sussex (01273) 515527. Email: elizhowe@dsl.pipex.com

CONTENTS

Front Cover: The end of the SBP near Rye.

Title Page: Looking to the spire of Burstow church.

Back Cover: The bridge over the Rother near Bodiam.

ABOUT THE AUTHOR

David Bathurst was born in 1959 and has enjoyed writing and walking throughout his adult life. He has walked all the complete official long-distance footpaths of Great Britain including the South West Coast Path, the Pennine Way and Offa's Dyke Path, and he has also walked the entire south coast of England, his guides to the Sussex and Kent coasts being published by SB Publications in 2002 and 2007 respectively. By profession David is a solicitor and legal adviser to magistrates in Chichester and Worthing. He is married to Susan and has a daughter Jennifer. When not writing or walking he loves vintage sitcom, teashops, and singing. His most notable achievements have been the recital of the four Gospels from memory on a single day in 1998, the recital of the complete works of Gilbert & Sullivan from memory over 4 days in 2007, and reading the entire King James Bible over 6 days in August 2011. Among his scariest experiences is appearing as a contestant on The Weakest Link!

AUTHOR'S ACKNOWLEDGEMENTS

I would like to thank Lindsay Woods of SB Publications for her encouragement and support; Liz Howe for her splendid work in preparing the text for printing; and my wife Susan and daughter Jennifer for their love and forbearance.

INTRODUCTION

The Sussex Border Path, opened in 1989, is not the longest "name path" that passes through Sussex - the whopping 620-mile long Monarch's Way bears that distinction - but it is the longest path that starts and finishes within Sussex. It's a curious animal, too, in that not only is there a linear route which starts at one end of Sussex and finishes at the other, but there is also a spur route which links with the linear route. The total distance covered is around 150 miles.

The name of the path really says it all; the linear route follows close to or beside the entire border of Sussex, West and East, with its neighbouring counties of Hampshire, Surrey and Kent. The spur route runs close to or beside the border between West Sussex and East Sussex(or at its bottom end, the unitary authority of Brighton & Hove which was formerly part of East Sussex). The majority of the walking is in Sussex, but by no means all of it, with frequent incursions into neighbouring counties. The path certainly doesn't pretend to follow, to the letter, the actual border, which frequently runs through rivers and ditches and would be wholly impracticable to attempt. There's certainly no obvious feature, like Offa's Dyke, which will tell you the exact point where Sussex stops and another county begins, but at least you will know that generally speaking you are on the closest right of way to the border.

So, if you're not faithfully adhering to the border itself, why this walk? The answer perhaps lies in the route itself. It is an end-to-end walk round Sussex, and just about every aspect of Sussex scenery, is encompassed within its 150 plus miles. There's some coastal walking, a good deal of riverside and lakeside walking, some fine downland, Wealden and woodland tramping, sections of trails along disused railways, plenty of picturesque villages with historic buildings of immense interest, and one or two splendid old towns. Naturally, some sections are more interesting than others, but think of it like watching the rerun of all of a really good football match rather than edited highlights; there will be some dull moments but plenty that is really good and memorable, providing a whole which is satisfying and fulfilling. There is some extremely enjoyable walking contained in every section, and provided you are lucky with the weather, you will enjoy a rich mixture of sweeping views, refreshing waters and picturesque shady woodland, as well as a wealth of wildlife and plant life. This book offers a guide to walking the whole of the Sussex Border Path, including the spur route, hopefully enabling you, the reader, to really enjoy this end-to-end march round the edge of the beautiful counties of West and East Sussex. Once you've completed it, you can look back in satisfaction and truly say that you've walked right across Sussex which in itself is a very considerable achievement.

The walking is not difficult. There is the occasional stiff climb, but physically it is generally undemanding. You certainly will not require specialist walking equipment, but I do recommend stout shoes or light walking boots; in dry conditions, trainers will be more than adequate. How much of the SBP you walk at one go is entirely up to you. You may choose to do it all at once, perhaps staying at B & B's nearby, or you may prefer to complete the walk in day trips. There are no prizes for speed of completion, and indeed if you rush it you may miss a good deal. I have split the walk into sections of generally between 12 and 16 miles; for some walkers that will be a modest day's effort, while for others that will seem like a big ask. Included in the section preambles are suggestions as to how, if at all, the sections could be split further without recourse to cars or taxis, but if you are a reasonably fit walker you should have little difficulty in accomplishing each section within a single day. You should naturally listen carefully for the weather forecast and clothe and equip yourself accordingly. Sussex enjoys a balmier climate than most counties of Great Britain, and even in winter the days may be mild, but be mindful of the conditions and be prepared to reschedule your walk if necessary. I was fortunate to walk two sections of the SBP in snow, which had a magical effect on the surroundings, but it wasn't an easy journey home afterwards!

But while generally the SBP is a straightforward and not overtaxing proposition, there are two aspects that do present a particular challenge to the SBP walker, firstly route-finding and secondly lack of amenities for long stretches. I will deal with both in turn. Sadly, signage is very patchy in places, and while one should never attempt to navigate one's way along a long-distance path on the basis of signage alone, there are numerous points along the route where one could easily go wrong even with the aid of a map. Note particularly that in many places there is no Sussex Border Path sign but a plain Public Footpath or Public Bridleway sign; this does not necessarily mean you have lost the route, and indeed it's highly likely that you're on the correct route, as the SBP has tended to utilise existing rights of way rather than create new ones. Signage consists of a mixture of finger posts, some bearing the 1989 date of opening, and green badges affixed to gates and stiles, but there's no real consistency at all The current economic climate at the time of writing makes it unlikely that funding will be easily available to improve the standard of signage of the route, and I am not optimistic that by the time you read these words the situation will have improved. It seems to me there's a bit of a vicious circle; its poor signage means it isn't walked as much as it could be (indeed astonishingly, it doesn't appear in the most recent Trailwalker's Handbook, the supposedly definitive guide to name paths in Britain) and there's insufficient pressure from those who do walk it for anything to be done about making the signage better. It is for this reason that I have tried to highlight in the text areas where there is a high likelihood of your losing the route, and where the route description seems particularly detailed, you can take it that that is the reason. Even though I like to think my directions will suffice, you may still wish to equip yourself with a map so that you can see the context of your walk and possible "escape routes" should you get lost, and perhaps also a GPS device which can tell you precisely where you are at any given time.

Regarding amenities, while Sussex is hardly noted for its barren remote landscapes, there are still numerous sections of the route where you may go many miles between bus routes, pubs and shops. While all the sections into which I have divided the route below start and finish in or very near places that are served by public transport and offer at least one establishment where food is available, there is no guarantee of any amenities between the section start and finish points. The section between Wadhurst Station and Hawkhurst is an example of a section where there is nothing on offer whatsoever, either by way of refreshment or public transport, on the route itself. It is another sad sign of the times that the appearance of a village on the map is no guarantee whatever that you will find a shop, pub or café there. The section preambles make it clear what was available at the time of writing, to enable you to plan accordingly, but it is always essential to have supplies of food and drink with you. I have deliberately based the section divides around public transport availability, but you should note that many bus services don't run on Sundays or public holidays. My experience is that advertised bus services are very reliable - in all my fieldwork for this project I never once experienced a bus failing to turn up - but you may wish to have the reassurance of a mobile phone and the numbers of local taxi firms just in case. Bus operators and times can and do change, and it's advisable to consult the Internet or a library/tourist information office for clarification.

A note on abbreviations:
P = pub, C = café, S = shop.

A note on maps:
Please note that maps for sections 4-9 inclusive and 11 face east rather than north as you look at the page.

SUSSEX BORDER PATH - OVERVIEW

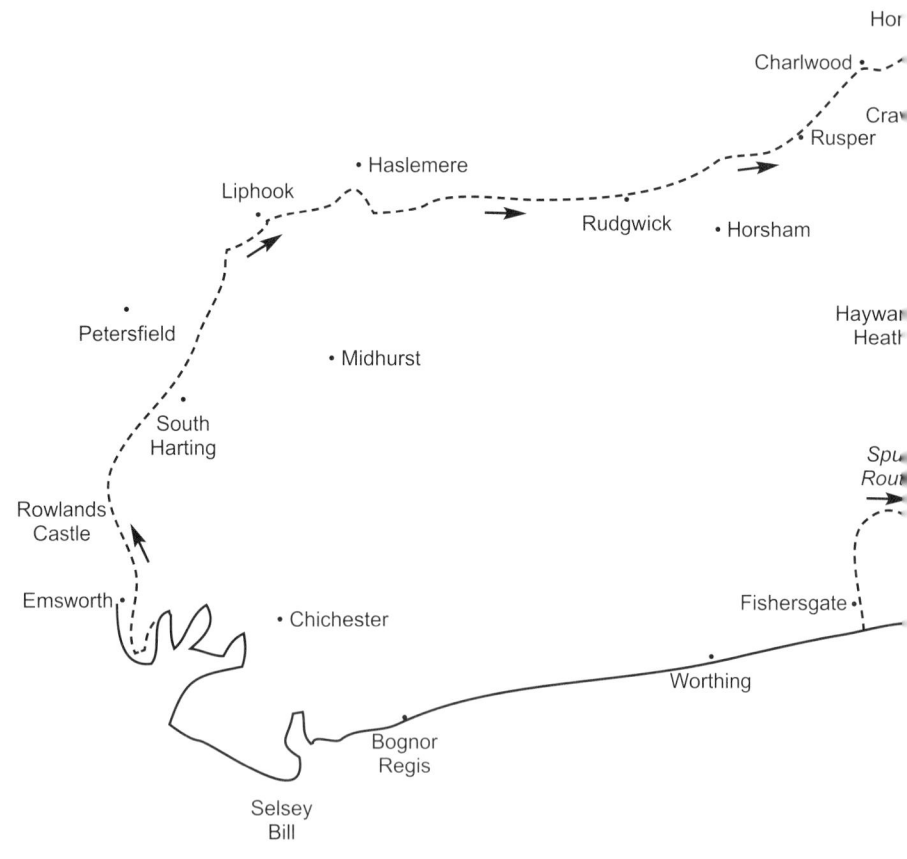

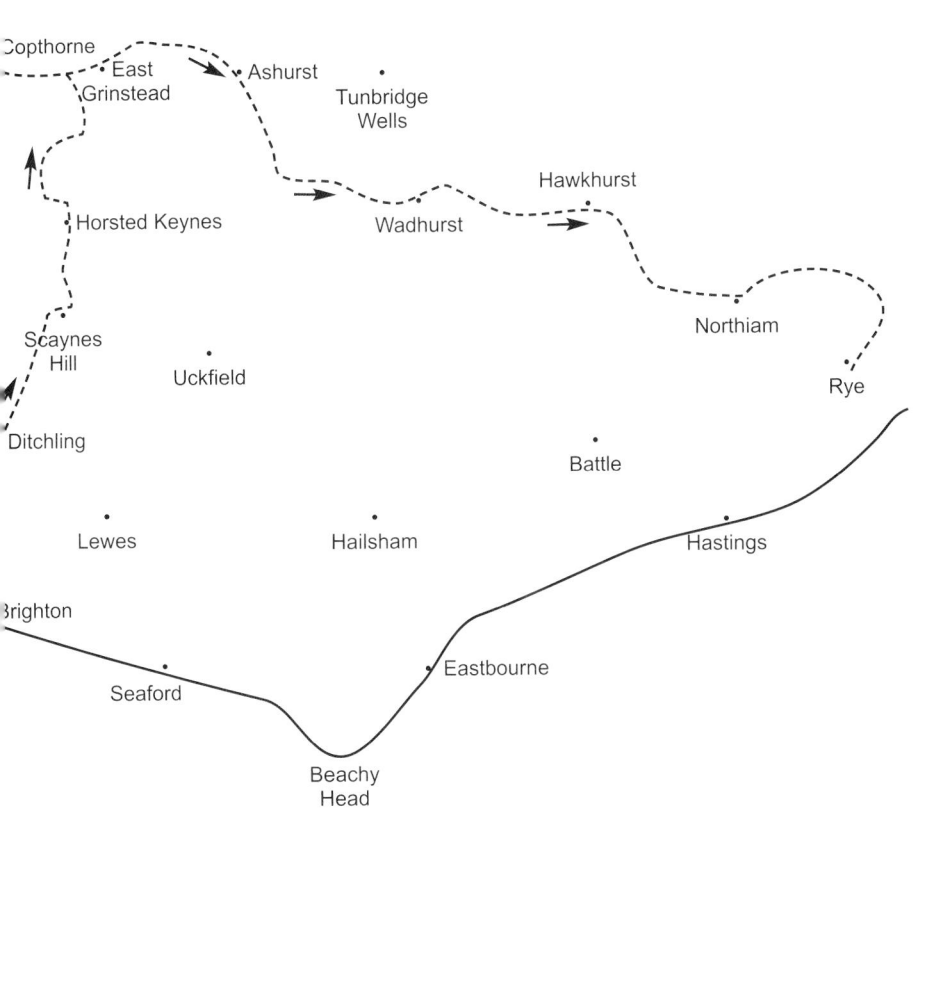

Copthorne
East
Grinstead
Ashurst
Tunbridge
Wells
Hawkhurst
Horsted Keynes
Wadhurst
Northiam
Scaynes
Hill
Uckfield
Rye
Ditchling
Battle
Lewes
Hailsham
Hastings
Brighton
Eastbourne
Seaford
Beachy
Head

SECTION 1 - **EMSWORTH - SLIPPER ROAD**

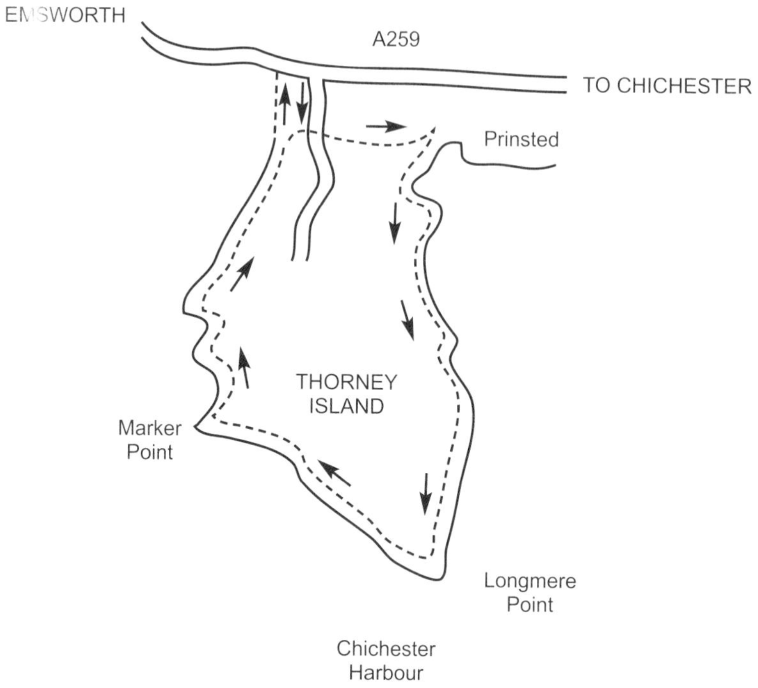

EMSWORTH

A259

TO CHICHESTER

Prinsted

THORNEY
ISLAND

Marker
Point

Longmere
Point

Chichester
Harbour

A tranquil November afternoon on Chichester Harbour near Prinsted

SECTION 1 - EMSWORTH - SLIPPER ROAD

Length:	8 miles.
Public transport:	Regular trains serving Emsworth on the Portsmouth-Chichester-Brighton line.
Refreshments:	Emsworth (P,C,S).
Overview:	This is a curious start to your Sussex Border Path (SBP) pilgrimage, in that you actually make no progress along the Sussex border at all, but simply describe a circle round Thorney Island! If you had to miss one section out this would be the logical one to lose. But it is a fine section with magnificent views across large parts of Sussex and Hampshire, and can comfortably be completed within half a day.

From Emsworth station walk southwards down to the roundabout junction with the A259 and turn left to follow beside it briefly. You pass between two ponds, and immediately beyond the ponds you go past Slipper Road which goes off to the right. Very shortly beyond the right turn into Slipper Road, you reach a signed footpath just short of the Sussex Brewery pub, this being the official start of the Sussex Border Path. Turn right to follow this footpath southwards, soon arriving at a field, and then follow the right-hand field edge, the path reasonably well defined. Continue in roughly the same southerly direction, but now keeping rougher vegetation to your left; you go forward to follow the extreme left-hand (east) edge of the Emsworth Yacht Harbour and soon arrive at a T-junction with a drive, and a signed footpath junction. Turn right and then almost immediately left along another drive with trees to the left, but look out very carefully in a couple of hundred yards or so for another signed path going off to the left. This is the Sussex Border Path although not signed as such. Take the path which proceeds clearly across a field eastwards to reach Thorney Road; cross straight over Thorney Road and follow a path heading just south of east, arriving at a driveway just short of Thornham Farm. Turn left to follow it, and very soon you reach a T-junction with a lane. Turn left again and very shortly you reach the water's edge at the south end of Prinsted. Climb up onto the signed embankment and bear right to begin your waterside clockwise walk round the edge of Thorney Island.
This is your first viewing of Chichester Harbour, and you will rarely be out of sight of it for the rest of this section. The harbour was formed after the last Ice Age, and is home to a huge array of seabirds including brent geese, shelducks, curlews, mergansers, dunlins,

Rest for the weary - looking back towards Prinsted

A well-signed path junction en route for Thorney Island

sandwich terns, ringed plovers, redshanks and oystercatchers, while plants include glasswort, sea lavender and sea purslane. Thorney Island, which you will follow all the way round, was a quiet sparsely populated agricultural community until the mid-1930s when a new air base was built here. The RAF remained until 1976 and the island then became an army base.

The going is now very easy indeed, proceeding in a predominantly southerly direction on an extremely good coastal path. You soon pass Thornham Marina and shortly beyond that, Prinsted Point and Thornham Point; you arrive at a gate where to proceed you will need to press a button and seek entry which will automatically be granted to you, and it's then plain sailing past Stanbury Point. You find yourself on the shore as you pass the island church of St Nicholas, and there is in fact a signed high water alternative just here. It's worth pausing to explore the church which dates back to around 1100; there are a number of Norman features in it, including a cylindrical font, as well as a modern pulpit designed by John Skelton. The massive tower was once used for the storage of contraband goods. The churchyard contains the graves of a number of soldiers and airmen killed in the Second World War.

Beyond the church the going is straightforward, as you proceed southwards to Longmere Point. You veer westwards here, bypassing Pilsey Island but enjoying superb views to East Head near the Witterings to the east, and Hayling Island to the west. Now you head north-westwards along a really good clear path, and it's fast easy walking all the way to Marker Point, the most westerly point of the island; you then veer sharply again to the right and now make your way northwards again towards Emsworth, which will remain in your sight all the rest of the way. There are great views ahead to the South Downs and Kingley Vale Nature Reserve. After negotiating a couple of mini-inlets it's a virtually straight run until you arrive at Emsworth Yacht Harbour. You need to ignore the wooden finger post signing a path hard right just before the Yacht Harbour, but you then do need to turn right as indicated by a metalled footpath sign once you are in the Yacht Harbour area, this footpath in fact a driveway between the boats. Shortly you reach a signed path junction, with two signed paths going off to the left very close to each other. You need to turn left along the first of these paths, along a wide driveway which soon reaches a brick building. Turn left here towards the marina, then veer right to walk northwards beside the marina, aiming for the gateway that allows access to Slipper Road. The road derives its name from Slipper Mill which was constructed in 1760, and subsequently converted into houses; historically Emsworth had a proud history of milling, the last mill closing as comparatively recently as 1970. Go into Slipper Road and continue in the same northerly direction to arrive back at the A259. You have effectively completed a giant circle. Now it's time to make some progress!

Along the straight and narrow - coming from Prinsted towards Thorney Island

Stretching ahead - the Sussex Border Path striking out towards Longmere Point

SECTION 2 - **SLIPPER ROAD (EMSWORTH) - HARTING**

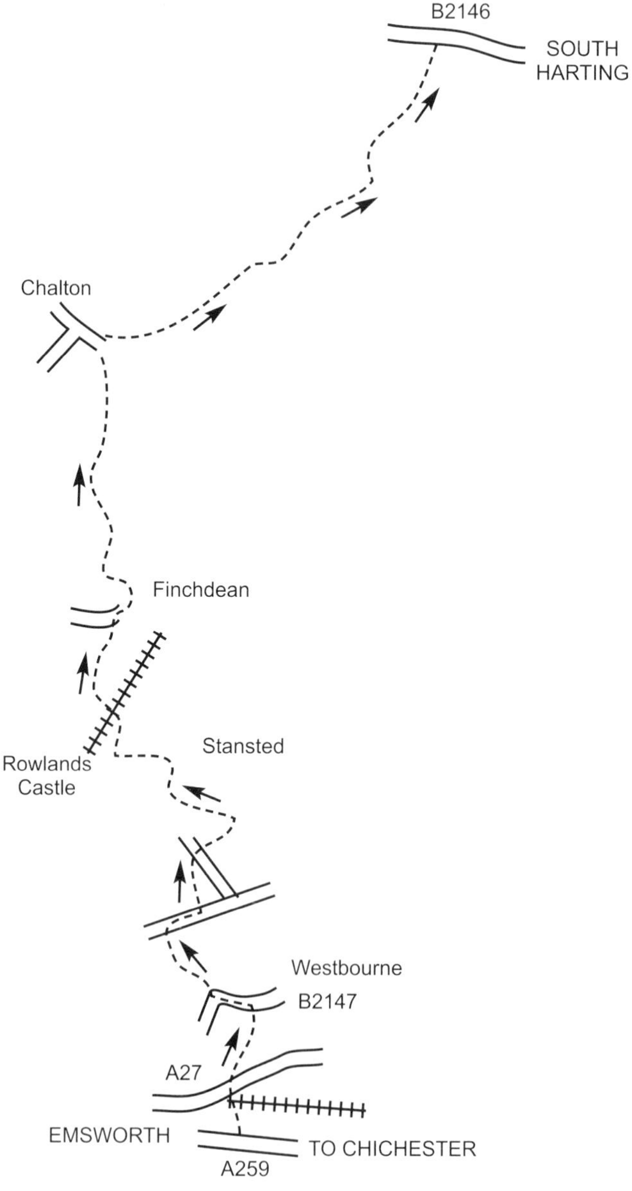

B2146

SOUTH
HARTING

Chalton

Finchdean

Rowlands
Castle

Stansted

Westbourne
B2147

A27

EMSWORTH   TO CHICHESTER
          A259

SECTION 2 - **SLIPPER ROAD (EMSWORTH) - HARTING**

Length:	12 miles.
Public transport:	Regular trains serving Rowlands Castle on the London-Portsmouth line; regular buses serving Harting on the Petersfield-Chichester route.
Refreshments:	Rowlands Castle (P,C,S); Finchdean (P); Chalton (P); South Harting (P,S).
Overview:	A section of great variety and superb scenery, with the walk from Finchdean to Chalton a particular delight. The woodland section between Chalton and Harting can be confusing, so watch the signposts carefully. The journey could conveniently be broken at Rowlands Castle.

Cross straight over the A259 into Lumley Road, at last seeing an SBP signpost! Walk up Lumley Road under the railway bridge, just beyond which you approach a large house and PRIVATE sign. Turn left along a signed SBP path, crossing a stream and going forward to a T-junction of paths; bear hard right here and follow the path, soon passing under the A27 and following a path close to the left edge of a field. Near to the top left corner of the field leave it and walk along a path parallel with it, soon arriving at the B2147. Turn left to follow it to a roundabout, and at the roundabout bear right

Looking down on the pretty church of Idsworth above Chalton

Two well-defined sections of the SBP above Finchdean

onto Redlands Lane; as the road bends left, at a nameplate for Redlands Lane, carry straight on northwards along a path which widens and rises to a T-junction with Long Copse Lane. Turn left here.

Follow the lane briefly until it bends sharply left. At the left bend there are two turnings to the right: ignore the first, leading to Hollybank House, but take the next one on the right, a lovely path through Hollybank Woods where there's a splendid variety of bird life to be found including tits, bats, warblers and woodpeckers, and plants include early purple orchids. Rise to Emsworth Common Road, and turn right to follow it, soon passing a sign warning of horses crossing in 90 yards. At the horse crossing point turn left onto a path through woods, dropping gently then veering left and continuing through woods, rising to Woodberry Lane. Go straight over Woodberry Lane onto a track and follow it for just under half a mile, passing through the hamlet of Stubbermere. Beyond the hamlet, look out for an imposing red brick house which is to your right (you can't miss it!), and after another 150 yards turn left along a signed footpath into the Holme Farm complex. You kink right then left round the side of the barn then follow a good path across fields, soon passing just to the left of woodland, and shortly beyond the woods you reach a junction of paths with Horsepasture Farm immediately ahead.

Don't go forward to the farm, but bear right at this junction up a rather faint path through a field, rising slightly, soon reaching woodland to the right and then left. You've now reached one of the scenic highlights of this section, the broad so-called Avenue linking Stansted House and Rowlands Castle, and by looking to the right here you can clearly see Stansted House. The original building was a Royal hunting lodge which in 1686 was replaced by a house designed by William Talman and extended in the late 18th century. The house was very badly damaged by fire in 1900 and largely rebuilt by Sir Reginald Blomfield although parts of the earlier construction remain. The grounds were laid out in the early 18th century and the avenue of beech trees has been described as one of the best in England. In 1724 Daniel Defoe commented on his ability to see from the west end of the house right down to the town and harbour of Portsmouth and ships at Spithead. While you may not get that clarity, it's worth pausing to enjoy the view which on a half-decent day is still magnificent. You reach a path junction in the middle of the grassy carpet between the lines of trees, turning left to follow a clear path along it, going forward into and through woodland and descending to arrive at Finchdean Road just outside Rowlands Castle. The SBP turns right up Finchdean Road and doesn't visit Rowlands Castle, but it's certainly worth detouring into the village with its excellent range of amenities. The village takes its name from a motte-and-bailey castle situated to the east of the present settlement; it came briefly into the spotlight in 1994 when Stage 5 of the Tour de France cycle race passed through it.

Having turned up Finchdean Road, you soon reach a signed path going off to the left and reassuring SBP disc, the path going off by house no 73. Walk up the path, going uphill and veering shortly right to cross over the railway. Go forward along a clear green path north-westwards over fields, veering left to arrive at a lane (note the PRIVATE sign to the right) and following it very briefly until a junction of paths just before a lovely thatched house. Turn right here, keeping the house to the left, and follow the narrow Wellsworth Lane, veering right then continuing north-eastwards on a lovely path across open fields. You descend through the trees to reach a road, turning right and dropping down to Finchdean village. Finchdean, originally Finchesdene and meaning either "valley of the finch, or of a man called Finc,' is a delightful village, with the bonus of the pretty George pub to help quench thirsts.

Turn left at the Staunton Way signpost more or less opposite the pub, and follow this road briefly, soon reaching a junction with a road going off hard right at no 1A. Just past no 1A turn right onto a path going immediately parallel with the road on a left-hand field edge; at the far bottom end of the field, turn right as signed (Staunton Way) and walk uphill along a lovely path with views to Idsworth church. Keep walking uphill, arriving at an area of trees which you pass through, and on emerging you'll see a pylon and clump of trees at the top of the hill ahead. The main path veers sharp right and descends, but you turn left here on the Staunton Way path and follow it, avoiding a subsequent turning to the left and continuing on a clear path on a left-hand field edge. It's now straightforward going, following the clear path through fields over Chalton Hill, and enjoying the best views so far. You pass through a gap in a boundary hedge then begin to dip down, crossing a field to a hedge and a PRIVATE sign. Just before the sign you turn left onto a path which drops down and veers right, crossing a stile and going through a gate to enter the churchyard of Chalton church. Chalton - not to be confused with Charlton! - means "farmstead on chalk" and was formerly known as Cealctun. It's certainly worth exploring the church, which dates back to the 13th century and boasts a particularly fine east window.

Having visited the church, drop down to the road by the half timbered and thatched Red Lion pub, another good refreshment opportunity! Turn right onto the road, but almost at once reach another road junction and bear right onto the road signed Idsworth. Follow the road, soon passing (but not taking) a signed Byway and almost immediately beyond, turn left onto a signed path, going in a straight line eastwards as signed over the field ahead then veering slightly left and dropping very steeply to reach a road. Turn left then very briefly right onto a path which crosses the railway, then beyond the railway you carry on in a straight line, reaching a

Straight and true - the approach to Chalton

The pretty church of Chalton

road which comes in from the right. Go straight on into Harris Lane, avoiding a signed turning to Ditcham Park School, and continue up Harris Lane, soon entering woodland. Follow on through the woods on an obvious path, passing a signpost with an SBP disc on it. Follow the path up to roughly a mile from the point where you joined Harris Lane. Now you need to concentrate and keep your wits about you! Having walked the mile or so from Harris Lane, you'll see the path bending slightly left and at this point you reach a path junction with four fingers on it, three bridleway and one footpath. Here you need to leave the wide path, turning right here and then immediately left onto a narrow footpath heading north-eastwards. It begins rather unpromisingly but continues through woodland uphill, close to the edge of the woods. On gaining height, it widens out and the signage becomes better. Follow the wider path for a couple of hundred yards, then reach a signed path forking left from the wider path, and join this left forking path. Continue through the woods, going over a crossing path, and arrive at a T-junction, bearing right here and following this wider track to another T-junction where you turn left. Walk downhill to Foxcombe Farm and go forward along a metalled lane, rising slightly and crossing the South Downs Way. You're now "out of the wood" in every sense and you can relax! Drop downhill now and arrive at the B2146 South Harting-Petersfield road where this section ends; the SBP goes straight over, but by turning right and following the B2146 for less than half a mile you'll reach South Harting. Not only are there buses available to link with the rail network at Petersfield, but it is a large and attractive village, with thatched and timber-framed cottages and a splendid church containing nave walls which could be pre-Norman, an impressive Victorian tower and part of a 13th century effigy in the chancel.

SECTION 3 - **HARTING - HASLEMERE**

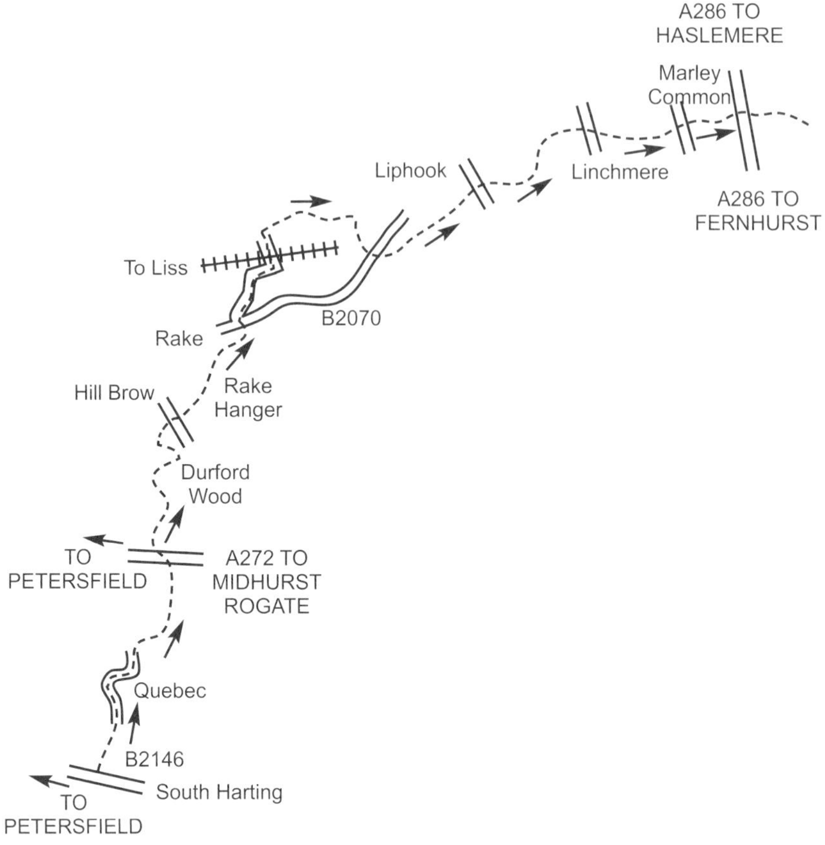

A286 TO
HASLEMERE

Marley
Common

Liphook

Linchmere

A286 TO
FERNHURST

To Liss

B2070

Rake

Hill Brow

Rake
Hanger

Durford
Wood

TO
PETERSFIELD

A272 TO
MIDHURST
ROGATE

Quebec

B2146

South Harting

TO
PETERSFIELD

The spire of South Harting church in the shade of the South Downs

SECTION 3 - **HARTING - HASLEMERE**

Length:	15 miles.
Public transport:	Regular trains serving Liphook and Haslemere on the London-Portsmouth line; regular buses serving Kingsley Green on the Midhurst-Haslemere route.
Refreshments:	Rake (P,S); Liphook (P,C,S).
Overview:	Woodland predominates in this section and the broad sweeping views you enjoyed in the previous section feel like a distant memory. Route-finding isn't always easy, especially when following woodland paths. Nonetheless, there are many enjoyable sections of woodland walking. The section can conveniently be split in two by stopping at Liphook, but bear in mind that neither Liphook nor Haslemere are "on route."

Having crossed straight over the B2146 continue on a signed path with SBP disc, rising and then walking parallel with the West Harting road through woods, your first taste of the large slice of woodland walking on this section. You drop down to the road in just under half a mile, turn very briefly right onto the road, and immediately reach a road junction. Turn left here and follow the road towards the hamlet of Quebec(no, you're not suddenly in Canada; interestingly there's another Quebec in England, in Durham, originally the name of a farmhouse). You go over a footpath crossing and arrive at another road junction. Fork right here and follow the road, ignoring a right fork into Collins Lane and going forward to a further junction. Bear left here and very shortly reach a stile and signed path going to the right. Cross the stile, bear left to follow the left-hand field edge initially parallel with the road, then swing round to the right to walk along the left-hand field edge, keeping woodland to the left. You cross another stile and arrive at a field with pylons running through the middle; follow the path direction as signed, walking beside wires that run at right angles to and cross the pylons. The path dips down then rises up to reach a stile and footbridge over some rough ground, and you then veer slightly right with the path to reach a junction with a lane, also a footpath, at Down Park Farm. Turn right onto the lane but then immediately left just before the farm buildings and follow a clear track just east of north, now on the Serpent Trail path, another long-distance path through Sussex which you'll see plenty more of during the ensuing miles. Follow the Serpent Trail path as signed(its signposting tends to be better than that of the SBP!), taking care to go straight on as the main track veers sharply right. Follow the left-hand field edge to the corner of woodland, reaching a lush green area with a house behind. Go over a stile, crossing the near side of this green area, and over another stile at the other end, bearing right onto a path which runs down between the sides of the old bridge. This bridge carried the railway which once linked Pulborough with Petersfield via Petworth and Midhurst, and closed in 1955. Go forward to a field and follow the left-hand field edge, going on to a muddy area in the shade of trees and dropping down to a fence with a meadow beyond. Cross the stile in the fence and bear half-right, aiming for and going through a gate which leads to a bridge over the Rother. Beyond the Rother follow a track which goes forward to the A272. There are buses along this stretch of road, plying the route between Midhurst and Petersfield, but although there is no bus stop just here, you may be lucky enough to flag one down! Turn left to follow the A272, but turn shortly right up the approach road to Durleighmarsh Farm. Keep the farm buildings to your left and continue up the obvious path, soon reaching a junction, and take the signed path left, going in a northerly direction with open country to your right and left. As you reach woodland, look out carefully for and take a signed bridlepath forking off to your right which enters and then winds its way through Durford Wood; its course is very obvious and well signed, and this is a really enjoyable woodland walk. Veering north-east, then north-west, then north-east again, you go forward to arrive at the Hill Brow-Rogate road. Turn left to follow this road briefly, then turn shortly right at the next road junction and proceed quite steeply downhill. Very shortly the road bends left; soon after the left bend the Serpent Trail goes off to the right (but not you!), and soon after that the road bends

Snow and mist below the South Downs near Rogate

right. The SBP goes off to the left on a path at this bend, but at the time of writing it wasn't signed, so could easily be missed. Once you've joined the path, though, its course is obvious, proceeding north-eastwards through Rake Hanger; don't be beguiled by what appears to be a path along the bottom of the slope but keep to the path a little up the slope to the left, soon being joined by a path coming in from the left. Note a number of ponds to the right, adding to the beauty of the scene. I was fortunate enough to walk this section on a sunny December morning following two days of snow, and although it was a long icy bus ride to reach it, the sight of the snow carpeting the trees made every minute of the journey worthwhile. Rake Hanger is now a Site of Special Scientific Interest with a fine variety of trees including sessile oak, silver birch, whitebeam, rowan and several species of lichen. You rise gently to arrive at another road, turning left along it to reach the B2070 at Rake. This was once the main A3 London-Portsmouth road but despite its demotion, it is a busy road, so cross with care.

Having crossed, turn right and almost immediately turn left along Brewells Lane. Follow the lane, forking shortly right at the next road junction (there is a lovely old fashioned signpost here, worth a camera shot) and continuing along the lane to another road junction at Brewells Farm. Turn right here - the road going to the right only seems to present itself at the last moment - and follow the road to a T-junction signed No Through Road to the left. You do turn left here, and go forward to cross the railway, then almost immediately beyond the railway crossing you reach a fork junction. Don't go hard right (a sign advises you it's private anyway) or straight on, but take the middle signed path going half-right. This is a lovely path which passes the houses of Langley then skirts the edge of woodland, going downhill to arrive at another multi-path junction. Take the right-hand path, which goes forward to arrive at a junction with a road which goes towards Forest Mere. It's important to take the signed path going right here and now follow the clear path heading eastwards along the edge of the woods, passing close to Folly Pond which is to the left although you don't see much of the pond! You reach a junction with a driveway going off to Home Park to your right, and you then need to fork right along a signed path which almost immediately swings southwards along the edge of the woods, going forward to pass back underneath the railway. Immediately beyond the railway turn left as signed along a path between fields, soon arriving at a T-junction of paths where you turn right and enter woodland, going on along a clear path which at once swings to the left (southwards), goes through a gate and continues through the woods to a path crossroads. Turn left here along the signed Serpent Trail path which returns you to the B2070. It's been a lot of walking to avoid having to stick to the B2070!

Turn left onto the B2070, passing a welcome pub, and follow it very briefly until you reach the next road junction on the right, signed Milland and Iping. Turn right onto this road, almost immediately reaching a road T-junction; go straight over onto a signed footpath which now heads north-eastwards in a straight line, across Liphook golf course, so do be careful and give way to golfers. (Or do what I did and wait till the course is covered with snow so there won't be any golfers!) You go over a crossing driveway and continue in the same direction, but beyond a path junction your obvious and well-signed path veers a little more to the left, a clear path coming in from the right. Simply continue on this path until, just over a mile from where you left the B2070, you approach another road, and as you get within sight of it, there's an (at the time of writing, unsigned) left fork which you follow uphill to arrive at the road. You are now very close to the village of Liphook, and by turning left to follow this road you will shortly arrive there. This is an obvious stopping place if you've either had enough for the day or you fancy some refreshment before carrying on, as there are no more opportunities on this section.

At the road crossing the SBP goes more or less straight over the road onto Highfield Lane. Almost immediately after joining Highfield Lane, turn right onto a path which at the time of writing was signed Serpent Trail and New Lipchis Way but not SBP, even though this is the correct SBP route; SBP walkers must at times feel very unloved! Now it's time to sit up and take notice, as it were, because route-finding now gets tricky. The path is initially very clear through the woods, but becomes less distinct, so be sure to follow the New Lipchis Way and SBP signs (the Serpent Trail goes away to the right shortly). There is a point, just under half a mile from Highfield Lane, where the New Lipchis Way takes a definite veer to the left; veer left with the New Lipchis Way which the SBP follows, but shortly you reach another path junction where the New Lipchis Way goes off sharply to the right. Don't take this right turn but go straight on as signed through the woods. Look out for, and take, the signed bridleway away from what appears to be the main path, steeply downhill into a valley along which a bridleway runs. The map tells you to go straight over, uphill then veering left along a yellow arrow-signed footpath through the woods and dropping back down to the valley bridleway. However the signposting directs you left onto the valley bridleway which goes along the edge of woodland to be reunited with the map route close to a beautifully sited house, Lower Brookham. Beyond the house you veer right and it is now very important for you to stick to the bridle route, ignoring paths going away to the left. Continuing just south of east, then veering just north of east, you go uphill on a woodland path which is initially narrow but then widens. Fortunately (and just as well!!) the SBP signing hereabouts is excellent, so follow that and you will soon arrive at a road just north-west of Linchmere. It now gets a lot easier. Turn right onto this road, ignoring the next road going off to the right, but turning left at the next road junction advising that Haslemere is 3 miles away. However almost immediately after joining this road, turn right onto a signed bridleway which follows a clear and obvious course, with good SBP signposting as you go. You walk initially just south of east then veer in a more easterly direction and in about a mile from the road junction referred to just above, you arrive at a road coming in from the right, at Marley House. Continue along the road in the same easterly direction but as the road veers away to the left, you carry straight on along the signed path through the woods, going forward over a crossing track and shortly arriving at

Like icing on a Christmas cake: snow capped vegetation in Rogate Hanger

another road. This is as close as you get to the Hampshire/Surrey border, a little to the north; the SBP is now following close to the border with Surrey, and Hampshire is left behind, a sign of the progress you are making. Turn left at the road and then very shortly right along the approach track to the Marley Common car park. Beyond the car park continue in the same direction across the common, ignoring a number of paths going off to the left; thankfully the SBP signposting is very good, so you shouldn't go wrong. Marley Common, like its neighbour Black Down (see below) is a mixture of wood and heath and is particularly rich in bird life including the nuthatch, woodcock, nightjar, crossbill, meadow pipit, yellowhammer and woodpecker. In just under half a mile you'll see the Serpent Trail signed to the left, away from the main path, and you need to take this signed path, following the Serpent Trail (SBP not signposted just here)very steeply downhill through the woods, aiming for the houses below. You arrive at a residential road, and although the Serpent Trail is signed straight over along an alleyway, you should turn left along the road which takes you downhill to the A286 just north of Kingsley Green with bus stops here enabling you to go to Haslemere (nearside), Midhurst and Chichester (far side).

However if you're proceeding along the SBP, go straight over the A286 onto Fernden Lane. The road shortly bends sharply left and you need to bend left with it, but as it bends right almost immediately you need to go straight on along a signed path which proceeds beside houses, veering right and continuing to a T-junction of paths. Turn right here, very shortly reaching another path junction where you turn left and follow a signed path along what feels like a driveway. Pass to the right of the gates leading to private housing and continue in the same easterly direction along a much narrower woodland path, which soon veers left to cross a narrow bridge over a watery area and arrives at a junction with Bell Vale Lane. The section ends here. Your way forward along the SBP is right, along Bell Vale Lane (signed Valewood House). However if you wish to detour on foot to Haslemere, turn left and then almost immediately right signed The Stables. Shortly you fork left along a signed public byway and follow it uphill to arrive at a road; turn left and almost immediately right along a narrow path which drops down, over a crossing lane and steeply down to the B2131. Turn left and you will soon reach the centre of Haslemere.

A wintry scene between Rake and Liphook

Snow enhances the predominantly wooded scenery between Harting and Haslemere

SECTION 4 - **HASLEMERE - RUDGWICK**

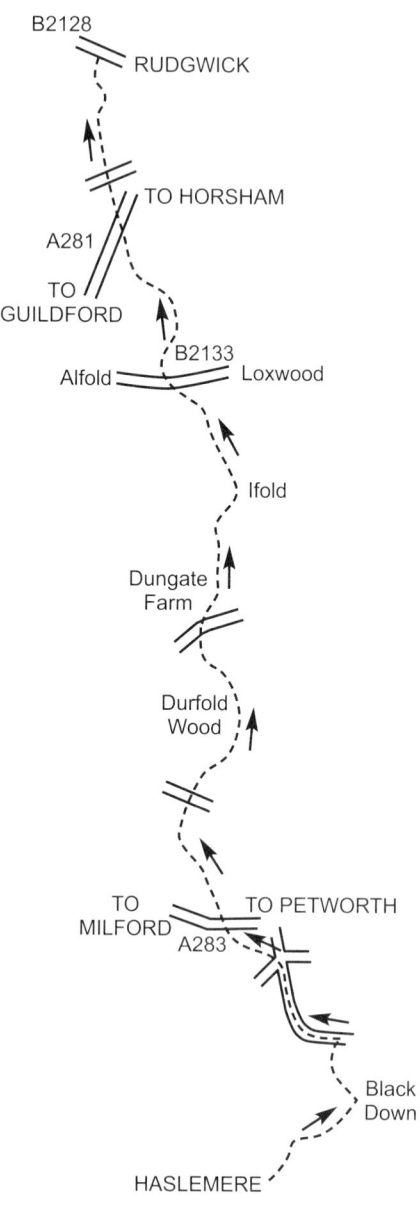

B2128

RUDGWICK

TO HORSHAM

A281

TO
GUILDFORD

B2133

Alfold

Loxwood

Ifold

Dungate
Farm

Durfold
Wood

TO
MILFORD

TO PETWORTH

A283

Black
Down

HASLEMERE

SECTION 4 - HASLEMERE - RUDGWICK

Length:	13 miles.
Public transport:	Regular buses serving Rudgwick on the Horsham-Guildford route.
Refreshments:	B2133 crossing (P); Rudgwick (P,C,S).
Overview:	This section starts with a bang, the magnificent ascent of Black Down, the summit of West Sussex. Thereafter, the walking is pleasant rather than spectacular, but reasonably easy to follow for the most part. Note that there is no possibility of being able to split the journey as there are no public transport options on the route.

Follow Bell Vale Lane briefly south-westwards, veering southwards, but shortly you reach footpaths coming in from the left. Turn hard left here to follow the signed SBP which proceeds briefly northwards, then in a couple of hundred yards executes a spectacular hairpin bend to the right and proceeds uphill, going forward, just east of south, to cross the middle of a field, aiming for a gate at the far end. Go through the gate and continue into woodland, going uphill to reach another gate, veering slightly right (southwards) and then continuing as signed along a path through the woods. The path then veers left, going straight over a bridleway crossroads, and now goes uphill onto the slopes of Black Down, part of the Greensand Ridge of the north Weald and once an extensive heath created by grazing. You reach a

A snowy approach to Blackdown

The summit of Blackdown just off the SBP

major path junction, with the Serpent Trail path signed to the right, but you need to bear left - not the first left path going off downhill, but the next one, going north-eastwards, continuing to gain height. As you reach the top, a path comes in from the right(1), and here the SBP simply carries on north-eastwards. However, this is the closest you get to the summit of Sussex, at its highest point 919ft above sea level; the best views are from the Temple of the Winds, reached by turning right at (1) above and simply heading southwards for just over half a mile, and I strongly recommend you make this detour as there's nothing better to follow on this section.

Having made the detour return to point (1) and resume your SBP walk, heading north-eastwards, soon losing height. You pass a seat and viewing point which is to the right, and come within sight of what looks like a trig point and information board, but just before this you need to bear right onto a thin path which goes quite steeply downhill to reach Tennyson's Lane. Don't join the lane but simply skirt to the right of it, continuing in the same direction along a driveway signed for Aldworth House. If this sounds familiar, it was built around 1869 for Alfred, Lord Tennyson, who lived here for the last 20 years of his life and wrote much of Idylls Of The King, based on Arthurian legend, in its back garden. The house is private and not open to the public. Very soon after joining the driveway you fork right onto a signed path which soon bends sharply right and then sharply left, going steeply downhill. You come to within sight of the buildings of Roundhurst but just before reaching them, turn left onto a signed (yellow arrow) footpath which brings you down to a road. Turn left to follow the road, then at the next road junction bear right along Jay's Lane, a metalled road which goes steeply downhill at first then follows quite a bending course to reach a T-junction with Jobson's Lane. Turn left along this lane to another T-junction, where you need to go straight over onto a signed path that proceeds north-eastwards through a strip of woodland with fields to the right and left. Be careful, at the footbridge over a stream, to take the right of the two forking paths beyond. The path begins to gain height and goes forward to a drive which in turn reaches the A283. Cross with immense care and turn left to reach the junction of the A283 with the B2131 going off to the left.

Immediately opposite this road junction, bear right along a signed path on a right-hand field edge. You veer gently left then in a couple of hundred yards after leaving the road, bear right along a signed footpath which enters woodland and proceeds straightforwardly through the woods. You emerge from the woods and continue along the right-hand field edge, arriving at another patch of woodland. Take care to follow the path leading half-right (not half-left) into the woods, going quite sharply downhill and rising to reach a crossing track. Turn right and then very shortly left along a signed path which resumes a clear course along the right-hand field edge, initially north-eastwards then veering gently south-eastwards and going forward to a junction with a minor road. Turn left and then immediately right as signed, but at the "Beware of the Bull" sign you need to turn sharply right along a narrow but clear path, with wooden fencing protecting you

The SBP meets the Downs Link

from the bull in the fields that are to the left! Shortly the path veers left and you now return to the familiar field edge walking, dropping downhill to cross over some horse gallops - looking out carefully for fast-moving horses.

Your path transfers its allegiance to the left-hand edge of adjacent fields, and the going continues to be straightforward as you proceed south-eastwards along the north fringes of Manorhill Copse. Beyond this copse, fields take over to the right but a much larger area of woodland comes in from the left. Your path continues along the right-hand fringe of this woodland, heading eastwards, and actually enters woodland just above Winkins Woods Farm which you can see to your right. Emerging, you now veer north-eastwards with the same pattern of fields to the right and woods to the left. Carefully observing the signposts, but continuing in the same direction along the well-marked path, you now enter woodland which goes forward to pass a number of buildings, your path now becoming a clearer wider track. You cross a driveway and continue along a narrower path beyond to reach the Plaistow-Dunsfold road at Dungate Farm.

Cross straight over the road onto a driveway, but almost immediately bear right as signed and follow the signed path just south of east along the left-hand field edge, aiming for a large area of woodland. You enter the woods then very shortly look out for, and take, a signed path going off to the left. It soon veers right and continues through thick woodland to another path junction with a signed footpath going to the left. Ignore this but go straight on - a silver SBP plaque on the wooden post here will confirm - and almost immediately veer quite sharply left. You drop downhill to cross a stream by a plank bridge, ascend and then drop down to a second stream, also crossed by a plank bridge. Go forward to reach a T-junction with a track, turning left and very soon reaching a wide crossing track; go straight over this and shortly reach a corner of the woodland with fields and the buildings of Lee House Farm to the half-right. Turn right here and now go forward along a wide farm track, heading south-eastwards through woodland.

You now follow this track for just over half a mile, then need to look out for the Forestry Commission "Hog Wood" sign on the right; shortly beyond this sign you'll see a large modern house on the left with fields beyond it. Just before this modern house you'll see a signed path leaving the farm track on the left. Follow this path which now proceeds

The impressive Kings Head pub at Rudgwick

pleasantly along a right-hand field edge keeping Oxencroft Copse to the right. You cross Barberry Bridge, taking your path over the Wey & Arun Junction Canal. The canal opened in 1816 and remained operational until 1871; it is being gradually restored to its former glory, with some fine stretches of water and restored locks and bridges, but some dry and dilapidated sections were still in evidence at the time of writing. Having crossed the canal you then enter woodland and go over another name path, the Wey South Path. The going is now very straightforward, along a clear path which heads north-eastwards and arrives at the buildings of Oakhurst Farm. You are signed round to the right of the farm buildings along a wide track which drops downhill and then continues along Oakhurst Lane to reach a junction with the B2133 Loxwood Road. The pretty village of Loxwood is just under a mile away to the right; however you may not feel the need to detour, as the Sir Roger Tichborne pub, the only on-route refreshment opportunity between Haslemere and Rudgwick, is immediately beside you on the left. Turn left from Oakhurst Lane onto Loxwood Road and follow it briefly.

Just a short way up Loxwood Road, turn right into Pigbush Lane - your first road walking for some time. You proceed past houses and then out into the countryside again, veering right, south-eastwards. At some farm buildings about half a mile from the B2133 the road peters out but you carry straight on along a clear path. The path enters woodland and veers to the left, then veers right and goes forward to reach a junction with a byway. At the time of writing this byway was wide and clearly defined but extremely wet and boggy (made no pleasanter for me by falling snow and icy temperatures!), so do take care. Turn left to follow it, but shortly you reach another path junction with the SBP forking off to the right. Follow this fork path, shortly reaching a fork junction of tracks. Don't be tempted by either, but instead follow the signed bridleway between the two tracks. It's then a very straightforward walk just north of east along a straight well-defined bridlepath through woodland and then past the buildings of Rikkyo School. You cross a driveway and shortly beyond it veer slightly left then slightly right to arrive at the A281, which is a very busy road indeed. Cross straight over with great care, turn right along the verge and then bear immediately left along Hillhouse Lane, following it to its end. At the T-junction at the end, go straight over onto a path which skirts the edge of woodland immediately adjacent to Well Grove. Gaining height, you emerge at a field and, continuing in the same direction, go straight over the field, negotiating a couple of quite tight kissing gates!

You enter an area of woodland, and, still heading fractionally north of east, you pass through the wood, overlapping briefly with the Downs Link and passing over Baynards Tunnel. This is part of the former railway that linked Horsham with Guildford, closing in 1965, but now mostly converted into a path and forming a major part of the Downs Link route. Sadly the tunnel is closed and not on the Downs Link! You go over a footpath crossroads at the end of the wood, the SBP clearly signed heading out into the field beyond, heading still just north of east. At the next field boundary you veer to the right and follow the right-hand field edge which skirts the edge of some claypit workings,

A cluster of old buildings in Rudgwick

veering first south-east then north-east and reaching the corner of some woodland. The path then veers to the right through the top edge of the woods. Ignoring paths going away to the left, you now proceed south-eastwards as signed across a field to reach the main street at Rudgwick. Turn right and walk the short distance down to the church, marking the end of this section. The SBP goes almost up to the church then along the right-hand side of it, but you will surely want to take advantage of the amenities of Rudgwick which are a little further down the village street. Its name meaning "dwelling or farm on a ridge," it's a pretty village of tile-hung cottages, and the church of Holy Trinity is certainly worth exploring; although there has been a church here since Norman times, the south nave wall surviving from that period, it is chiefly 14th century albeit with an early 13th century squat west tower which boasts huge corner buttresses. There's also a 12th century font made of Sussex marble.

SECTION 5 - **RUDGWICK - CHARLWOOD**

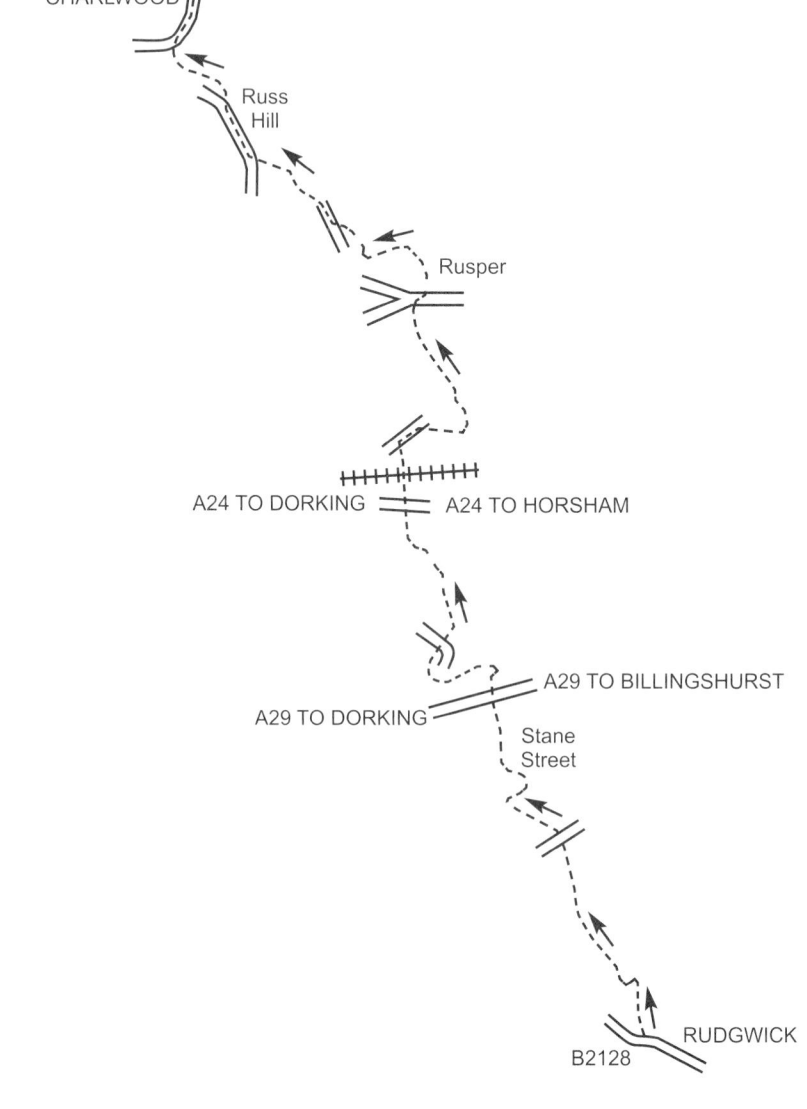

CHARLWOOD

Russ
Hill

Rusper

A24 TO DORKING   A24 TO HORSHAM

A29 TO BILLINGSHURST

A29 TO DORKING
Stane
Street

RUDGWICK
B2128

SECTION 5 - **RUDGWICK - CHARLWOOD**

Length:	15 miles.
Public transport:	Regular buses serving Charlwood on the Crawley circular route via Crawley, Ifield and Three Bridges, all of which are on the main London Victoria-Horsham railway line.
Refreshments:	Friday Street(P); Rusper (P,S); Charlwood (P,C,S).
Overview:	Again this is pleasant rather than dramatic walking, but with a couple of splendid woodland interludes and the delightful village of Rusper en route (although there is no bus service to speak of from Rusper so if you decide to split the walk here you're likely to need a taxi!). Aircraft noise becomes very intrusive as you progress.

To follow the SBP from Rudgwick, go up the Rudgwick church path, past the right of the church, and walk forward to a gate. Go through the gate, along the path, and straight on through the field, the path very clear; you arrive at a T-junction with a lane and bear left along the lane. You arrive at a crossroads of tracks, where some OS mapping suggests you should turn left, but I suggest you proceed as signed, going straight over, passing through a field and going forward into a wood, keeping a pond to the right. The path becomes a lane and arrives at a T-junction with another lane; turn left here, then at the next path junction turn right and follow a clear field path. Drop slightly to a T-junction with a metalled lane, bearing left and following this lane as it goes on to Bury St Austens Farm. Kink left slightly to pass through the complex but keep in broadly the same direction (just north of east), then, following the SBP sign, continue along the concrete path for half a mile past Ridge Farm and on to a road junction. Turn left then immediately right past Honeywood House; I was diverted a little left because of falling tiles but continue on an obvious path through woods north-eastwards to a road. Don't join the road but turn hard right immediately down Monks Lane, following it out of woods to a T-junction at Monks Farm. Bear left and follow the path uphill towards Ruckmans, but in just over a quarter of a mile, bear right onto a signed bridleway, a lovely peaceful section of path. Follow it, then at the fork at the edge of the wood, take the right-hand path, signed SBP, which takes you to the A29. Cross straight over with great care along a lane, veering right to Denne Farm going straight through the complex. Beyond it, veer a little left, up to bridlepath junction(1), where there is a sign indicating the SBP is to the right.

The mapping of the SBP suggests that you should turn left, going downhill into a meadow (a SBP sign soon reassures you), going on to the edge of a wood. Bear right as signed but look out for two gates on left; take the second (at an angle) and the path beyond it, not very clear through the woods but keeping a pond to the left and arriving at a gate. Go through it and observe the blue bridlepath arrows going just west of north to a road. Turn right onto the road (Weare Street), firstly south-eastwards, veering north-eastwards, going right into the signed Smugglers Lane. Follow it as it heads south-east, and veers eastwards at a footpath junction(2). However you could take an alternative route to (2) in obedience to the SBP sign at (1); it is actually prettier. To do so, follow this bridlepath from (1) south-eastwards, veering southwards then more south-eastwards again, passing a tiny redbrick house which is to your left. You continue along a very clear path through the trees, emerging and proceeding uphill on a right-hand field edge, then at the top corner of the

An idyllic cottage in the pretty village of Rusper

field veer sharply right along a more clearly defined path through the trees. The path reaches another sharp bend to the right before widening and heading towards a road but at this bend you need to turn hard left along a signed path heading northwards along a right-hand field edge. It veers north-westwards, still on the field edge, and passes through a narrow strip of woodland, then continues along the right-hand field edge to the top corner of the field. Observing the signpost, you then enter the wood and drop down steeply to cross Tickfold Gill by a footbridge. It's a super interlude in an otherwise unremarkable stretch, and it's worth following this "alternative" route for that only. You climb steeply up the other side then continuing to follow the footpath direction arrows, head just west of north along a clear path through the trees to reach Smugglers Lane at (2) above.

Whichever way you've reached Smugglers Lane continue eastwards along it for roughly half a mile past Oakdale Farm and go on uphill to Wattlehurst Farm. Immediately beyond bear left on a signed path through fields then, keeping woodland to the left, go through a gate into woodland, come out the other side heading north-eastwards, then veer north-westwards up to Bonnetts; an SBP sign reassures you, and you go forward onto a lane. You soon reach a junction of lanes, turning right and heading in a roughly easterly direction to the A24. Cross this road with great care - it's the main Dorking-Horsham road but single carriageway here - and bear left then immediately right along a clear path downhill over a railway, going straight on down to Rusper Road. Bear right onto the road, shortly crossing a brook, then immediately beyond the brook turn right off the road, onto a path heading southwards at an angle from the brook. Continue on along what is an obvious well signed path, just east of south, and drop downhill, to arrive at a T-junction of paths at the bottom. Turn left and go forward to reach a road, Friday Street, bearing left onto the road then shortly leaving the road by turning right just past the pub. A very well signposted section eastwards through farm fields keeping Porters Farm to right takes you forward into a meadow, dropping to a stream in a wood; bear left along a clear woodland path on the valley bottom, rising to emerge from the wood, keeping it to the right, and re-entering it at a spanking new sign bearing right. Once in the wood, turn almost immediately left onto a narrow path, taking care to follow the direction of the sign. It's a lovely stretch of woodland which will seem especially refreshing in summer. The path drops down using steps to a footbridge over a river; climb up the steps on the other side and go on uphill out of the wood, along a clear path to Rusper's main street onto which you turn right. Rusper, "place at the rough spar or beam of wood," contains a lovely mixture of half-timbered and tile-hung cottages, and a church which despite heavy Victorian restoration boasts a magnificent tower, chiefly 16th century. The village once boasted a Benedictine nunnery. It is an obvious stopping place but as stated above, public transport here is virtually non-existent; if you feel you've done enough for today(and this is a long section), a taxi may be your only option.

Following the main street you pass the church, then just beyond the pub but before a playpark to the left, turn left along a clear signed path, just north of east. After half a mile you reach a crossroads of paths at a wooded field boundary. The SBP is signed left, and goes forward to reach an area of woodland, veering firstly right then left, just west of north. It is particularly important not to get sucked away to the right, which you could very easily do; look out very carefully for the SBP signed path going off to the left, north-westwards through the wood. A useful marker is the stream you'll have skirted on reaching the woodland, and which you need to keep quite close to your left.

Assuming all is well, continue just west of north through the wood, reaching a T-junction with a path. Turn right to follow this path initially through the wood then north-eastwards on a left-hand field edge, with a wood to the left, going forward to a road. Go straight on along the road then as it bends sharply left continue along the right-hand field edge before going north-eastwards over the field away from the field boundary aiming for the buildings of Ivyhouse Farm. At the boundary before Ivyhouse Farm bear right along the left-hand field edge initially, then go on in a straight line as signed, passing immediately to the right of a pond, veering very slightly left with a wooded field boundary, unmapped, coming in from the right. Pass over a stile hard by the field boundary, and go forward to a road.

Turn right, pass the Russ Hill Hotel, (you could use a parallel field path) then as the road bends go straight on along a signed path cutting a corner. The path ends at a lane hard by the road; go straight on over as signed just to the left of Windacre Farm, onto another path. Follow the obvious path but observe the footpath signs carefully through the fields (there is only one path) and take care to veer slightly left from north-east to northwards. Veer right (north-eastwards) as signed to aim for Charlwood church, bearing right just before the church along a path, going forward to the village street, and bearing right again on to the main road. The section ends here, with buses available to Horsham and Crawley, but you may wish to linger awhile in the village, providing you can stand the aircraft noise. It apparently boasts more "crown post" timber-framed

Rusper's impressive parish church

A fine view from the SBP between Rusper and Charlwood

houses than any other village in Britain and is the home of the Lowfield Heath windmill; the village was the sometime home of David Sheppard, former England cricket captain and Bishop of Liverpool, and the motorcyclist Barry Sheene. The church of St Nicholas dates back to around 1080, the north aisle and tower base considered to be its oldest parts, and there are very fine wall paintings on the south wall which are believed to date from 1300.

SECTION 6 - **CHARLWOOD - EAST GRINSTEAD**

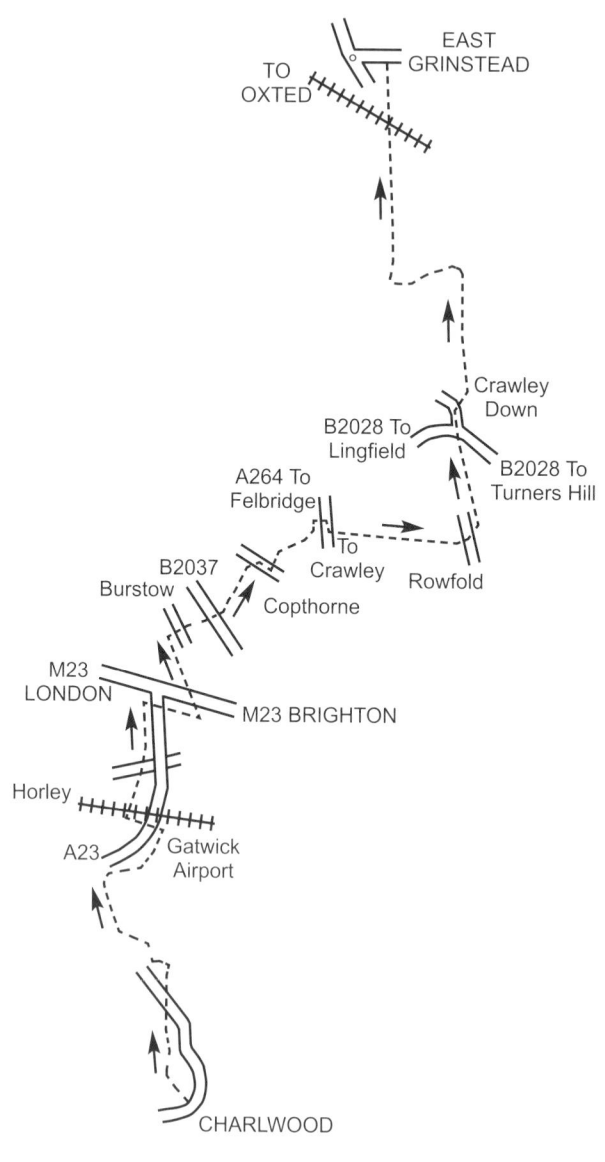

EAST
GRINSTEAD

TO
OXTED

Crawley
Down

B2028 To
Lingfield

A264 To
Felbridge

B2028 To
Turners Hill

To
Crawley

B2037

Rowfold

Burstow

Copthorne

M23
LONDON

M23 BRIGHTON

Horley

A23

Gatwick
Airport

CHARLWOOD

SECTION 6 - **CHARLWOOD - EAST GRINSTEAD**

Length:	12 miles.
Public transport:	Regular trains serving Horley on the London-Brighton line; regular buses from Copthorne to Crawley; regular buses serving Crawley Down on the Tunbridge Wells - Three Bridges route; regular trains from East Grinstead to Oxted, East Croydon and London.
Refreshments:	Horley (P,S); Copthorne (P,S); Crawley Down (P,S); Three Bridges (P,C,S).
Overview:	This section improves greatly as it goes on, beginning with the noise and fumes of Gatwick but providing some beautiful scenery beyond Copthorne and Crawley Down including some fine old railway walking towards East Grinstead. Route-finding is generally easy, and there are good opportunities to "split" the walk at both Copthorne and Crawley Down.

Having reached the main road at Charlwood, pass the shop, then bear left shortly afterwards on a lane signed to a school. Keep on, ignoring the school turning and passing the old Providence chapel, then go forward to a path crossroads; turn right to enjoy a very easy walk, straight ahead to the road. Cross the road, turn left, then turn shortly right along a signed path parallel with the road then right, away from it, to reach the river Mole, with Gatwick Airport immediately beyond the embankment behind it. Bear left to follow a riverside path, first above, then beside the river, veering east then north-east, all the way past the hotel, under a bridge over Mole, and forward to just short of the A23. Veer right along a path parallel with and on the near side of the A23 going south-east as far as a roundabout, and now things get very fiddly! Cross the first road, then go over the road leading to the North Terminal, and follow SBP signage straight on under the monorail. Beyond the monorail turn left to walk parallel with it then bear right as signed and go forward to reach Perimeter Road North. Turn left along it, keeping the police station to the left (if you think you're lost, ask for the police station!!). Follow Perimeter Road North to the very end, bear left, and follow the pedestrian route with clear SBP signage under the A23 and monorail then left as clearly signed. You pass under the M23, now walking parallel with the railway which is to the right. You reach a footbridge over the railway and turn right to cross over it, continuing on a path just north of east, veering gently right then more sharply right, before veering left (east) to

The lovely old church of Charlwood

Two of many attractive buildings in Charlwood

arrive at Balcombe Road. The SBP turns right here but by turning left and then left again into Victoria Road you will reach Horley and its useful station on the London-Brighton line.

However as stated the SBP turns right onto Balcombe Road. Follow it briefly almost to the M23 spur bridge, but just before it (beyond a driveway) turn left onto a signed path which goes parallel with the M23. Be careful not to get lured on to a muddy track through open ground by the M23 spur as you get near the minor road at the end, but having gone over one stile, cross over another and follow the very narrow path hard against the industrial works on the left to reach the road. Bear right onto Peeks Brook Lane, going under the M23 spur, and follow it southwards for just over half a mile, passing Fernhill Road coming in from the right. You then take the next left turn, Church Lane, and go forward to cross over the M23 and continue past an assembly of buildings. It has to be said that this is probably the worst bit of the whole SBP: not only are there no views to speak of, but it's extremely noisy as well.

When the tarmac road veers right, carry straight on north-eastwards along a path, and now things do improve considerably. You pass to the left of a lovely lake and arrive at Church Road, turning right to walk along Church Road through Burstow, "place by a fort or stronghold." It is certainly worth exploring the village church with features which date back to the 11th century; John Flamsteed, the first Astronomer Royal in 1675, was rector of Burstow from 1684 until his death in 1719, he is buried below the chancel, and he is commemorated by, appropriately enough, a star set in the large window above the altar. As the road bends 90 degrees left, go forward onto a signed path which crosses a field diagonally south-east, returning to the road - aim just left of the field corner to exit the field and regain the road. Turn right to follow the road to the B2037 Antlands Lane, crossing straight over, then of two forking signed paths take the left one, aiming for Newhouse Farm. Make for just to the right of a pond and you'll see a way forward to the farm buildings, turning immediately left and passing the top end of the pond, going forward through a gate to a field. Now walk through the field along the path as signposted, south-eastwards uphill, aiming just to the right of a prominent cream coloured house ahead. You'll then see a way through onto the road, Copthorne Bank. Turn right to follow the road, passing a pub which is on the right. Just past the pub the SBP turns left along Clay Hall Lane, but by continuing straight on you will soon reach Copthorne, a sprawling village and dormitory for Crawley. It's hardly worth the detour unless you are in urgent need of refreshment or transport.

Follow Clay Hall Lane just south of east for a little over a quarter of a mile to a right fork signed Roundabout Farm. Turn right here along what is initially a metalled driveway but as this swings to the left, you go straight on uphill along a path which can be very waterlogged. You arrive at the backs of houses and here turn left, following a path which becomes a lane alongside the houses, effectively the eastern end of Copthorne. The lane then swings right, keeping woodland to the left and houses to the right, and arrives at the A264. Cross carefully and on the other side you'll see signed paths going off south-east(hard left) and south-west (half-right). Follow the south-westward track, almost immediately crossing a track and walking through woodland, the path not always well-defined but reaching a T-junction with another track. Turn left to arrive almost immediately at a track crossroads, turning right and following signs for Keeper's Cottage. You follow a lane through the woods due south to Keepers Cottage, then continue just west of south as signed (the SBP signing is very good hereabouts) along a clear path, going forward to skirt the east side of Home Farm buildings. Ignoring paths going right and left, keep heading southwards, going downhill through woodlands and veering right then left to cross a stream and arrive at Rowfant House. This is a splendid building which was originally constructed in the late 16th century, probably for an ironmaster; although it was extensively restored in the 19th century it retains a number of late Elizabethan features. Turn right through the car park then, when you can go no further, left onto a driveway which passes the buildings and reaches a crossroads junction. Bear left as signed and shortly right, again as signed, going forward to Rowfant Lodge, then

veer left past the front of the house to reach Wallage Lane.

Turn left onto Wallage Lane and follow it briefly, until the signed turning to Rowfant Sawmills to the right. Immediately beyond this turning, and opposite a driveway going off to the left, turn right onto a narrow path which soon arrives at the Worth Way, the course of the Three Bridges-East Grinstead railway which opened in 1855 and was a victim of the Beeching axe in 1967. You can now relax for a while, enjoying a straightforward walk along the old line for roughly a mile, passing over Wallage Lane and then under Turners Hill Road (the only overbridge in this mile). Shortly beyond the overbridge you reach a gate. Immediately before the gate, bear right along a path shortly taking you to Grange Road, and you turn left here to follow Grange Road downhill to Crawley Down. This is another sprawling dormitory village, but there is a

The splendid east window in Burstow church

48

useful row of shops to the left, and there's a good bus service if you're flagging. On reaching the crossroads at the bottom of the hill, turn right along Sandhill Lane, going uphill and then bearing round to the left, eastwards, becoming Burleigh Lane when Sandhill Lane goes off to the right. Continue eastwards along Burleigh Lane to its end, at the buildings of Burleigh House, then join a footpath along the left side of Burleigh House, maintaining your easterly direction. The views are really lovely at this point, and the noise of Gatwick seems a long way back. Continuing eastwards along an obvious path, you gently drop downhill through a succession of fields to cross a stream, then keep going in roughly the same direction uphill, initially through trees then emerging along a clear path through more fields. Look out carefully for the buildings of Tilkhurst Farm which now loom up to your right, just under a mile from

Looking to the spire of Burstow church

Burleigh House, and when you get level with these you reach a footpath junction, turning left and heading just west of north on a clear green path. You soon reach a signpost directing you straight on: do NOT veer right onto the wider track just beyond the signpost but keep going north-westwards on a thinner path, passing the left edge of a pond and going forward to arrive back at the Worth Way (the old railway). There'll be no more route-finding problems on this section! Turn right to follow it for a mile and a half, reaching East Grinstead; at the far end of the upper station car park to your right, bear right as signed across the footbridge of the existing line. You arrive in the lower station car park. Bear slightly left as signed "Forest Way" alongside the station/Sainsbury's approach road to reach a roundabout. The section ends here, and you're now spoilt for choice, with a supermarket and café ready to welcome and revive you, and trains waiting to speed you home.

The old railway line between Crawley Down and East Grinstead, part of the Forest Way

A chance for SPB walkers to pick up a bit of speed - delightfully straightforward walking en route for East Grinstead

SECTION 7 - **EAST GRINSTEAD - ASHURST**

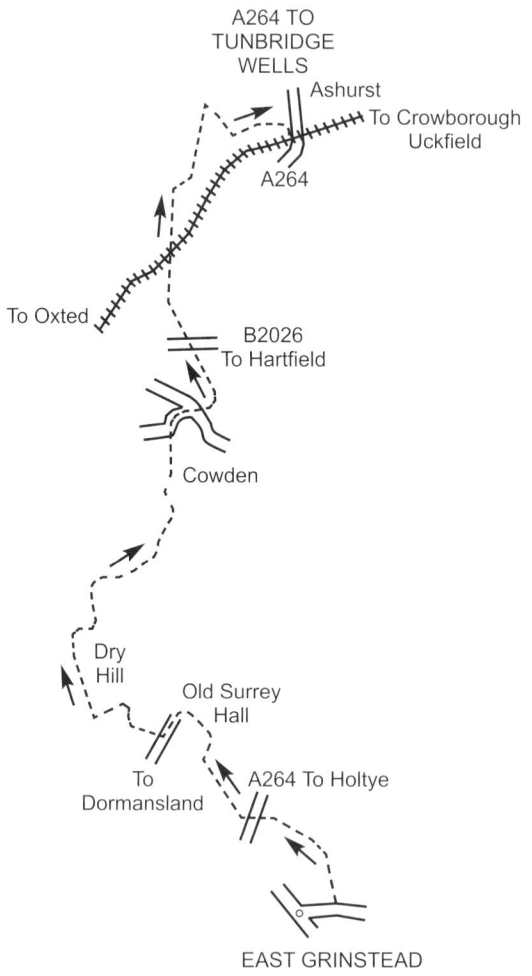

A264 TO
TUNBRIDGE
WELLS
Ashurst
To Crowborough
Uckfield
A264

To Oxted
B2026
To Hartfield

Cowden

Dry
Hill
Old Surrey
Hall
To
Dormansland
A264 To Holtye

EAST GRINSTEAD

SECTION 7 - **EAST GRINSTEAD - ASHURST**

Length:	10 miles.
Public transport:	Regular trains serving Ashurst on the Oxted-Uckfield line.
Refreshments:	Cowden (P).
Overview:	This is a shorter but surprisingly remote section, with no towns or villages of particular note, and there is some fiddly route-finding. However there are some really scenic sections and spectacular views, so pack a picnic, choose a good day for it, and enjoy. Please note that there are no easy ways of splitting this walk into two.

From the station/Sainsbury's approach road at East Grinstead, walk down to and go straight over the roundabout along Railway Approach, eschewing the two arms of the A22 going away to the left. Follow Railway Approach to its end and turn right onto London Road, East Grinstead's main thoroughfare - your first town actually on the SBP. It's an attractive town, too, with a number of fine half-timbered buildings in its main street including Cromwell House and Clarendon House, and the late 18th century church of St Swithun has eight bells, the largest peal in Sussex. Arguably the town's most impressive secular building is the stone-built Sackville College, founded in 1617, and also worth seeing is St Margaret's Convent, established in the 19th century, with a particularly fine chapel. Having reached London Road, very shortly turn left onto King Street and immediately right up a metalled alleyway, Institute Walk; follow this in a straight line, going over Cantelupe Road, noting the prominent tower of St Swithun's to your right. Go straight on into De La Warr Road to arrive at a T-junction with the B2110 College Lane, turning left to follow it. Cross over the A22 by a bridge, and pass the right turning to Estcots Drive immediately beyond the bridge. Just past Estcots Drive turn right along an SBP-signed lane which heads downhill past some lovely houses, and becomes a narrow path. Keeping the houses to the right you continue on the obvious narrow path, veering gently from eastwards to north-eastwards and then veering left, more sharply north-eastwards, to keep the houses to the right: don't go forward between the houses. Now continuing north-eastwards on the clear path, ignoring paths going off to the left, go on through Ashplats Wood, walking uphill and veering right to reach a lane. Turn left to follow the lane northwards to reach the A264 Holtye Road; cross over and bear left to follow this briefly, very soon bearing right onto a signed path heading just east of north, keeping a fence to the right and enjoying lovely views. When the fence ends the path immediately stops. You need to bear half-right and having

crossed a grassy area you'll see a path dropping steeply downhill through rough grass. You arrive at a wide strip of green: don't bear right onto this but go forward into the trees of Blackhatch Wood, picking up a path on roughly the same line as the path through the rough grass, heading just east of north. Soon a signpost in the trees reassures you, and you turn right here as directed, almost immediately reaching another footpath sign and a large field. You now say farewell to West Sussex for what will be the last time, and re-enter Surrey. Cross the field, heading north-eastwards along what is a lovely clear path through the middle of it, arriving at a wide crossing track; go over it as signed, and enter another field, following the right-hand field edge round

An unusual signpost beside the SBP at East Grinstead

until you see a sign directing you right, through the trees along a wider path. Follow this wider path to a T-junction at which you turn right and go up to arrive at another junction. Turn right at this one as well, and follow it down to within sight of the superb timber-framed buildings of Old Surrey Hall. It is believed that the buildings date back to the 15th century; during World War 2 the then owners turned it into a maternity home rather than let it be requisitioned by the Army. Don't go forward onto the forecourt of the Hall, but just before it turn left uphill along a signed narrow path of grass and mud (the West Sussex/East Sussex border is just south of here). Soon you reach a fork: the temptation is to carry on, but you need to turn left, shortly reaching another junction where you turn right along an attractive path which rises, veering left and providing lovely views. It's a rather rough path but is at least clear, veering gently left, northwards, to arrive at a road, Hollow Lane.

Turn left to go along Hollow Lane for just over a quarter of a mile, reaching the hamlet of Two Houses, the road kinking slightly right here and then almost immediately left. At this second kink, turn right along a signed path, initially between fences and through a gate by a house which is on the left. Continue on an obvious path downhill, veering left, looking very carefully for and taking a signed path going away to the right. This heads eastwards then just south of east through a large field, arriving at a drive leading to Upper Stonehurst Farm. Turn right to follow the lane briefly, but then shortly bear left as signed north-westwards along a right-hand field edge path, going uphill. Although this is fiddly and labour-intensive, it's worth it, as it's the prelude to some splendid high-level walking. Continuing in the same north-westerly direction you go forward to a metalled track which reaches a T-junction of farm tracks at Old Lodge Farm. Turn right and follow a clear metalled track, Moon's Lane, which heads north-eastwards with super views, bending slightly right and arriving at the extensive buildings of Dry Hill Farm. The track bends sharply right: beyond the right bend, don't go straight on but bear left, eastwards, along a wide track. Shortly the signed Vanguard Way goes off to the left, but you continue eastwards, emerging from the trees but then shortly - a quarter of a mile or so from Dry Hill Farm - entering another area of woodland. Almost immediately you reach a path junction with blue "Explore" logos on the signpost. Here you cross from Surrey into Kent, and for the rest of the walk will be either in Kent or East Sussex. Walking in Kent you'll notice how the SBP is marked with round green discs but the

A broad field followed by the SBP between East Grinstead and Cowden

marking is spasmodic in places and you can't rely on it! Turn right at this path junction and follow a lovely path through Jules Wood, with the embankment of Dry Hill Reservoir just away to your right. You veer left, south-eastwards, deeper into the woods and soon reach a fork of paths. You take the left-hand one, soon emerging from the woods to allow quite fantastic views across to the North Downs. Your path skirts the south end of the field, with woods to the right, veering right and arriving at another path junction with a path going off to the right, south-eastwards.

Follow this path, initially through the woods and then along a right-hand field edge to arrive at a fork junction with horseriders being directed to fork right onto the bridlepath. You however fork left, along a clear path south-eastwards across a field. At the next field boundary you veer very slightly right along a left-hand field edge to reach a path crossroads with metal gates on each side. Go through both metal gates, going straight on through the wood to emerge shortly at another gate, turning right as signed to follow a right-hand field edge just west of south. The path isn't too clear on the ground but at the corner of the field you veer left to continue along the right-hand field edge south-eastwards. You proceed initially past woodland that's to your right, but go on to a field boundary where you are signed and veer slightly right. There's a superb view from here; make the most of it because you're now coming off the hills and won't get back up this high for many more miles. Follow the right-hand field edge downhill, aiming for the right-hand edge of Clay's Wood further down, and, when you get to the wood, proceed along the path as it skirts the woodland before veering sharp left to pass through the wood. Emerging from the wood you veer right and now enjoy a very easy walk downhill through the field ahead, south-eastwards. You can really get up some speed here! You come to a field boundary and can now see the splendid buildings of Waystrode Manor, a Tudor manor house, ahead of you. There's a choice of paths through the field ahead; you need to take the left one of the two, aiming for just left of the manor. You now drop down very steeply to cross a stream, then climb very steeply up the other side, steps helping you as you ascend through the woods and go forward along a path which widens and becomes a driveway, with the manor to the right. Continue along the driveway to reach a road. Join the road, carrying on effectively in the same direction, veering round to the right along North Street to reach the centre of the village of Cowden, "pasture for cows." The village, which had its own blast furnace from 1573 until sometime in the 18th century, boasts a 13th century parish church built of sandstone with a restored shingle-covered spire which was bomb damaged during World War 2.

On reaching the junction at the bottom of North Street, turn left and walk towards the church, but just before reaching it you turn right as signed, joining a path that takes you downhill, crossing a lane and arriving at Sweetwoods Park golf course. You reach a signed path junction, and you need to take the left path, almost immediately crossing a footbridge over a stream known as Kent Water which you'll now be following for some while. Shortly beyond the footbridge you reach another path junction, and you now turn left along the signed path heading just north of east, parallel with Kent Water and keeping it to your left. The character of the walk has completely changed; you've left the wooded hills behind and are now strolling through low-lying meadows, scenic but in a different way. Keep on through the meadows but when in a quarter of a mile you get level with the fine buildings of Sussex House Farm which are to your right, you need to switch banks, crossing a footbridge and now following the left bank of Kent Water. Heading north-eastwards, you now make easy progress to the B2026 Edenbridge-Hartfield road where you see signs marking entry to Kent on the left, and East Sussex on the right! Should you wish to stop here for the day you could turn left along the road to the crossroads and then right along a road to Cowden station, but it's a good mile away and you might feel you were better off ploughing on to Ashurst. The SBP though turns right to cross the bridge and then immediately left to proceed along the right bank of Kent Water again, negotiating a bit of obstacle course of stiles first; very shortly, however, you switch back over to the left bank! Now it's very fast, easy walking along the left bank for about half a mile before switching banks level with the Moat Farm complex. Back on the right bank, you now follow closely by Kent Water to the railway embankment, veering round to the right and parting from Kent Water to walk parallel with the railway then veering left to pass underneath it.

Having gone under the railway, veer right to cross the field and be reunited with the right bank of Kent Water, heading due east to cross Kent Water by a footbridge and now walking along the left bank, veering south-eastwards and arriving at a road. Turn

The stunning Old Surrey Hall near East Grinstead

right onto the road and almost immediately left, remaining on the left bank, keeping the road to the left, so you're walking between stream and road, the road further up the hillside. Following the clear path, you cross another golf course - be careful and give way to golfers - then, still heading south-eastwards, you pass under a line of pylons. It's all been quite straightforward since Cowden, but now you need to sit up and take notice as you're about to leave the sanctuary of Kent Water and signposting over the next half mile was, at the time of writing, pretty much non-existent. Barely 200 yards beyond the pylons, the path, keeping Kent Water to your right, veers round to the right, and reaches a footbridge over Kent Water. There is no signpost here. You need to cross this footbridge and now head south-westwards, directly away from the road with which you've been walking parallel. In front of you, directly in line with the footbridge, is Willett's Farm on the hillside. Aim directly for the farm buildings, reaching a wire fence, crossing using the insulator provided - again no signpost. Beyond the fence you join a very muddy track which passes the farm complex and becomes an exit road. Keep on it until immediately beyond the farm buildings you find yourself walking parallel with a hedge which is to the left. The hedge then veers left, away from the track, and it is here you need to exit the track, heading left past the corner of the hedge as it veers away, and proceed just east of south downhill. However at the time of writing there was no signposting here whatsoever. Your only "marker" is a small pond, which you keep just to your right as you begin your descent, following the line of a prominent white house on the hillside in the distance.

Walk downhill and you'll see the infant river Medway ahead; it's certainly a fine view, but if you had the same trouble getting here as I did, you may not necessarily be in the right frame of mind to enjoy it! A footpath sign at last reassures you and you now come down to the right bank of the river, following a crude and often very muddy path through the meadow, squeezing at one point between some trees and the water's edge, then keeping to the left-hand field edge. You pass underneath the railway again and now strike out south-westwards across the meadow to arrive at the A264. As the crow flies this is just over 5 miles from where you last saw it. You've covered getting on for twice that! Turn left to walk beside the A264 under the railway bridge and then turn right shortly along the road signposted to Ashurst station. You actually pass the station, with regular trains to Edenbridge, Oxted, East Croydon and London.

SBP signage can vary - sometimes arrows on stiles will be your only indicator that you're on the right track, sometimes you'll be lucky with an SBP plate!

SECTION 8 - **ASHURST - WADHURST STATION**

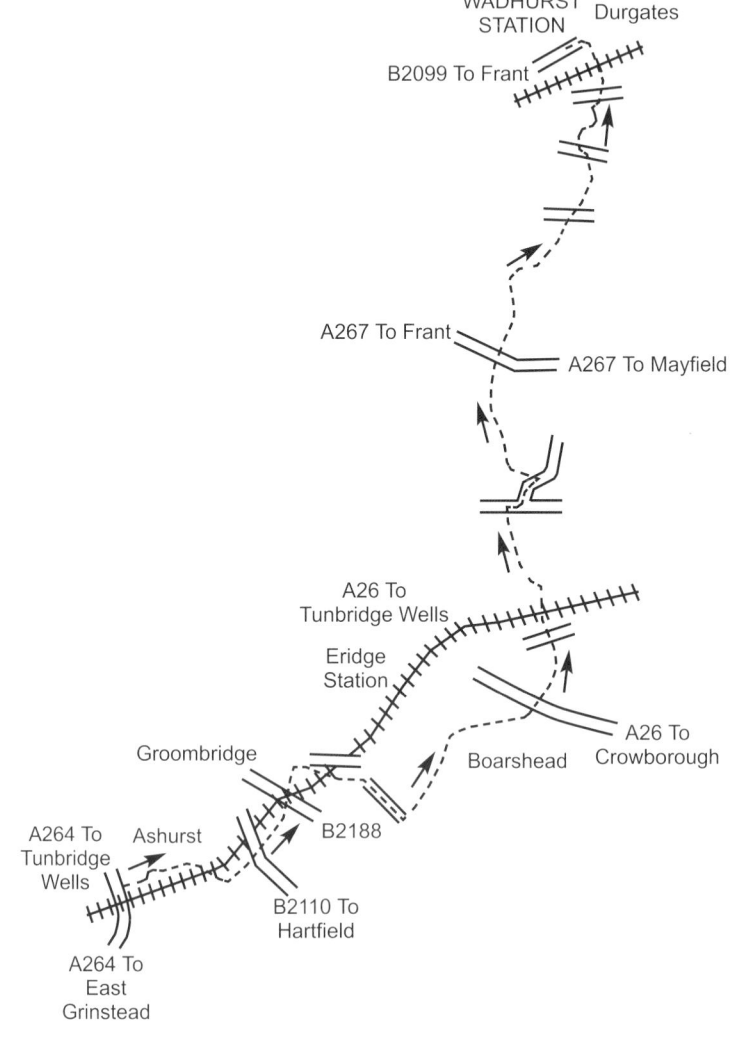

SECTION 8 - ASHURST - WADHURST STATION

Length:	14 miles.
Public transport:	Regular buses serving Groombridge on the Tunbridge Wells-Three Bridges route; regular buses serving Boarshead on the Tunbridge Wells-Brighton route; regular trains serving Wadhurst on the London-Hastings line.
Refreshments:	Groombridge (P,C,S); Boarshead (P); Durgates(P,S); Wadhurst (P,C,S).
Overview:	This section has a deceptively straightforward beginning; the remainder is demanding both physically and in terms of route-finding, but the scenery throughout is delightful, beginning with the Medway valley and then striking out across classic Wealden countryside. Boarshead offers the only realistic opportunity to split this walk.

Returning to the Ashurst station approach road, pass the station (unless of course you've used it!) and beyond it turn very shortly left. You climb briefly to a T-junction of paths, then head right, southwards past Jessup's Farm; just beyond the farm bear left as signed and climb, turning right at the top. Follow a good hillside path south-eastwards for a few hundred yards, losing height and arriving at a path junction with the Wealdway. Turn right here and descend to pass under the railway, then bear left as signed, going across the meadow to a footbridge beyond which you veer slightly right (just west of south) to reach a path crossroads. The Wealdway goes off to the right, while you turn left along a good clear track past Ham Farm to the B2110. Turn right to follow the road past the embankment of the old Three Bridges-Groombridge line, and immediately beyond turn hard left up a slipway onto the line itself - the Forest Way. This is another section of old railway, linking East Grinstead with Tunbridge Wells, opening in 1866 and closing exactly a century later. Follow it briefly, passing buildings which are to the left, and then a field also to the left. When you get almost level with houses on the far side of this field, look out for a stile on the near side of the field and a path coming up from the stile from the left to meet yours. Here you need to turn right, down a path going into the meadows below the old line to the right. Bear left and follow alongside the stream which takes you to Hendal Bridge and the B2188. Turn left to follow the road briefly then right as signed through a field - there's no path as such but walk diagonally across to meet the Forest Way after a few hundred yards as it swings left under a railway bridge. Now join and follow the Forest Way under the bridge and round to

This signpost between Ashurst and Groombridge has seen better days!

the right to arrive at a road. By turning left you'll soon reach Groombridge, with the widest range of amenities since East Grinstead. The prettiest part of Groombridge is some way beyond the actual village centre and is probably too far to detour.

However the SBP eschews Groombridge and turns right at this road junction. You pass some works which are to the right but very shortly bear right as signed, going forward to pass under the railway again. Beyond the railway you'll see a wide path going uphill through an open field. Don't take that one, but fork immediately left onto a path which goes more gently uphill, southwards, then along a hillside to enter between two strips of woodland. Veer south-westwards to follow a clear path along grass between the strips, going forward through woodland to reach a road at the hamlet of Mott's Mill. Join the road, heading in the same direction (south-west); it rises, and just before it bends right in a couple of hundred yards, bear left as signed onto a very well signed path which descends then rises, keeping woodland to the left initially. Beyond Rocks Farm, which is to the right, you emerge from the woods and now head south-eastwards through a succession of fields, passing just to the right of the buildings of Bullfinches and enjoying some really splendid views. There's then a lovely long descent through a field to a path crossroads and footbridge. You go straight over, following a right-hand field edge beside woodland, then swing from south-eastwards to south and reach another path crossroads, going straight over and descending to the corner of a wood. There's a stream crossing and a thoughtfully-provided seat here. Turn left to join a wide track which goes along the right side of the wood, uphill, to reach a T-junction of tracks. Turn right to follow a clear track past Renby Grange - the track looks private but it isn't - and swing south-eastwards to reach a T-junction with a road. Bear right and follow it downhill to a crossing of the A26.

Cross this busy road with care, straight over, then bear left up the slipway to arrive at the top end of a road. Join it but almost immediately turn left off it(by continuing along the road you'd reach the hamlet of Boarshead where there's a pub and there are buses towards Tunbridge Wells and Brighton). Your left turn off the road takes you onto a driveway which then bears right to Rocks Farm; to your left you can see the Bowles Rocks outdoor activity centre and may derive some free entertainment from watching some of the participants attempting the activities on offer. The path goes round the side of the farm bearing initially left then right, then beyond the farm turn left on a rerouting of the SBP, passing woodland which is to your right. You bear left at the field corner, then turn right just before another patch of woodland ahead. It's now a straightforward walk north-eastwards along a left-hand field edge, with good views to Bowles Rocks which are to your left. You descend to a road, cross straight over it, and follow the path in the same north-easterly direction keeping woods to your right. Beyond the woods you veer slightly right to pass under the railway again then from the bridge enter a field, proceeding along a right-hand field edge uphill straight on then round to the left till you get level with the Stitches Farm buildings to the right. Bear right to walk up to the farm buildings, looking back to get a lovely view of the railway and the woodland beyond; go across a north-south bridleway by the buildings, then veer slightly left as signed.

Excellent signposting now takes you north-eastwards, veering subtly left then subtly right, then a little left again through fields, before turning more sharply right and arriving at a road. Turn right onto it, then at the next road junction bear left, noting the wildlife verge. Follow the minor road towards Great Danegate but in just over a quarter of a mile, before reaching the buildings of Great Danegate, bear left on a clear signed path - it's quite wide and can be muddy. You drop downhill, then veer quite sharply right into woodland, veering left again then almost

A curious beast found near Groombridge

immediately right and following a clear path through the woods. It's all very well signed which is as well because the map is a little misleading. At one stage you pass through a metal gate, then over an active stream. The path narrows and reaches a T-junction where you are signed left, crossing another stream and emerging from the wood, now in the old Eridge deer park. This was reputedly the oldest enclosed deer park in England, mentioned in the Domesday Book; in the 19th century the Prince of Wales was a frequent visitor at shooting parties held in the park. Having emerged from the wood, bear right (east) as signed, keeping the woods to the right and following the northern fringe. When the woodland stops and fields take over to the right, you need to bear half-left uphill, keeping a strip of bracken and rather stumpy trees to your left as you climb. There's no real path here. As you get almost to the top, you reach a much larger tree, noticeably taller and more isolated, with a yellow arrow painted on it. A little beyond is a footpath sign. Look behind for a superb view of the countryside you've been following, then walk on eastwards in the direction of the arrow on the sign, arriving at a metalled kissing gate. Go through the gate and forward to the A267 Tunbridge Wells-Polegate road.

Cross the A267, turn right and then bear immediately left onto a lane taking you to Pococksgate Farm. As you reach the buildings turn left as signed, then shortly right, and walk along the left-hand field edge to a gate, going through that to pass through another gate, still along the left-hand field edge. Following in a straight line, you enter

Rolling Wealden countryside near Boarshead

Fine SBP scenery near Eridge

a further field where the hedge is set back, and here you need to veer half-right, losing height slightly and entering yet another field, where a yellow arrow each way reassures you. Don't plunge downhill.here but veer a little left to a half-hidden gate. Go through it and it's now much clearer walking just north of east, first on a left-hand field edge then through a field downhill to a footpath crossroads at the fine buildings of Lightlands. This is beautiful Wealden countryside with excellent views. At Lightlands you turn right along a very narrow path parallel with a drive, then, heading in the same south-easterly direction in obedience to the signage, drop downhill to cross a footbridge. You scramble up the other side through woods, emerging into a field where excellent signage takes you south-east to Earlye Farm. Follow the footpath signs carefully through the farm complex; beyond it you're signed right then left along a left-hand field edge quite steeply downhill. You enter woodland and go forward to a road.

Turn right to follow the road which immediately bends right and very shortly turn left onto a well signed path which soon crosses a stream, enters a wood and ascends. Emerging from the wood you keep it to your right initially then keep walking south-eastwards close to the left-hand edge of fields; the path signposting and the way ahead are very clear although in common with most of the A267-Wadhurst walk there's no mention of SBP at all. You then veer left - signs at the time of writing warned you not to feed the horses - and go forward to another road. Turn left onto the road and shortly right as signed, downhill through a field with woodland just to the right, entering the

A steep SBP climb between Eridge and Wadhurst

wood. You shortly emerge and veer left, keeping the woodland to your left, then veer right, still hugging the woodland. You arrive at a stream and here you bear left over a footbridge, very shortly right, left again by the buildings of Ravensdale Farm, and then right along a farm lane to reach a road. Cross straight over into Tapsell's Lane, heading eastwards, and as the lane shortly bends right, turn left as signed, north-eastwards along a path which heads for farm buildings and a gate; just before the gate, join a signed path on the left that continues in the same direction through woods, emerging into a field. From here, follow a clear path on down to the London-Hastings railway. Cross it as indicated with extreme care, climbing up the other side to the B2099. Wadhurst station is a short distance away to the left and Durgates and Wadhurst itself, your first proper amenity opportunities for miles, are to your right.

SECTION 9 - **WADHURST STATION - HAWKHURST (THE MOOR)**

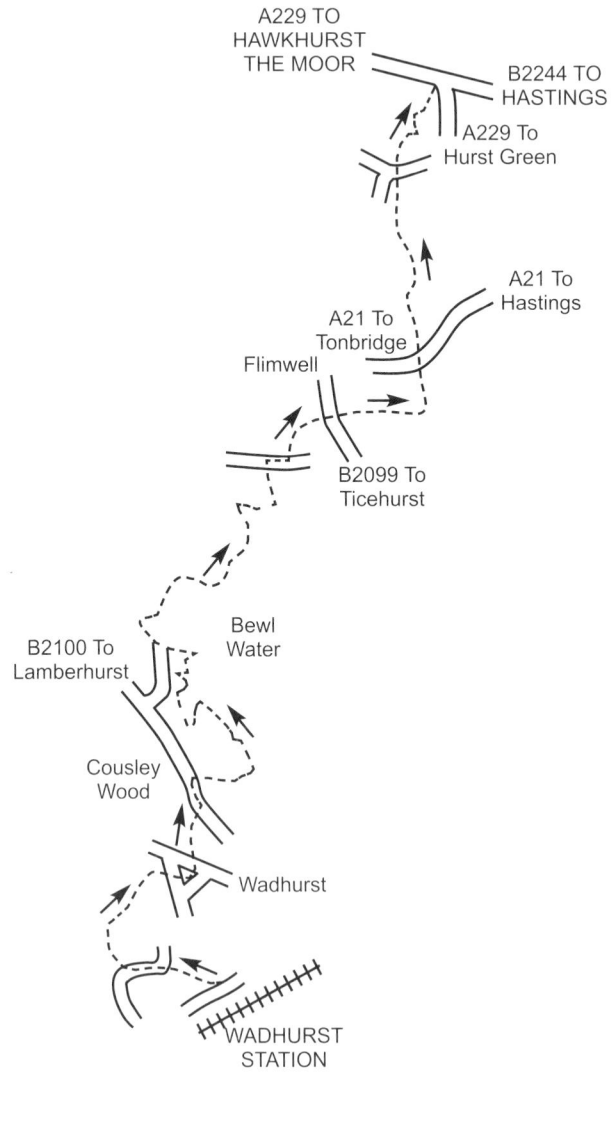

A229 TO
HAWKHURST
THE MOOR

B2244 TO
HASTINGS

A229 To
Hurst Green

A21 To
Hastings

A21 To
Tonbridge

Flimwell

B2099 To
Ticehurst

Bewl
Water

B2100 To
Lamberhurst

Cousley
Wood

Wadhurst

WADHURST
STATION

SECTION 9 - WADHURST STATION - HAWKHURST (THE MOOR)

Length:	12 miles.
Public Transport:	Regular buses serving Hawkhurst from Staplehurst.
Refreshments:	Cousley Wood (P), Hawkhurst (P,C,S).
Overview:	The first half of this walk is dominated by the delightful Bewl Water reservoir. The second half provides a final splendid high-level Wealden march, culminating in the pretty town of Hawkhurst with excellent amenities, but be warned that some of the walking is extremely fiddly with many excellent opportunities to get lost! There are no realistic possibilities of splitting this walk.

Having reached the B2099, cross straight over this road (if you're starting from Wadhurst station you'll need to backtrack a little) and then by the former pub and some adjoining houses turn very shortly right up a signed driveway. It veers right and almost at once you're then signed left along a path which heads north-westwards, passing through a private garden beside the houses of Rockrobin, arriving at a road. Turn right onto it then at the corner bear left onto a superbly surfaced path which heads just east of north then just west of north, entering woods then arriving at a road. Turn left onto the road and follow it first just east of north then just west of north, going uphill. As you enter woodland, bear right onto a signed driveway to Great Shoesmiths Farm, and on arriving at the farm you reach a gate; don't go forward to the farm buildings but turn hard right, almost doubling back on yourself. You veer sharply left and keeping a pond to the left, cross a meadow to reach a gate and a stream.

Cross over the stream then heading south-eastwards follow the clearly signed path through a field; continue south-eastwards through a much bigger field which could be muddy, although at least the signage remains very good! Go forward along a clear green path, before swinging sharp right and arriving at a driveway. Turn left onto it and follow it; it soon swings right and continues past some large houses, veering left to arrive at a road at Wood's Green. Bear left onto the road and walk down to a road T-junction. Turn right and very shortly turn left onto a signed path which looks as though it's someone's private drive but once through a gate it's a clear path south-eastwards, rising then proceeding along a right-hand field edge, veering right (don't fork away left) along a

wide grassy path to reach the
B2100 at Pell Green.
Turn left and follow the B2100 for
just over a quarter of a mile to
Cousley Wood. Just beyond the
Old Vine pub opposite the
Newbury Lane turning, bear right
along a signed lane, just west of
south, then as it bends sharply left,
go straight on uphill along the
track. At the top of the rise it bends
a little left, heading south-east.
Look out for a footpath signpost
pointing right along a right-hand
field edge, and take this path, going
quite steeply downhill. Continue
south-eastwards along the path,
keeping a boundary fence and
woods to the right, arriving at
another fence; cross it and bear left
as signed onto a path, heading
eastwards. You've now reached

Two views of lovely Bewl Water

Bewl Water, which you will have for company for the next five miles or so, and your path is good and clear, keeping the water close by to the right. Bewl Water is a reservoir, part of a project to increase water supplies in the area, and was completed in 1975; it is now the largest body of inland water in south-east England and is very popular as a sailing centre and for trout fishing. Note that as a major inlet is approached, the path cuts inland through trees; the SBP is shown on the map as following the water's edge all the way round, although when I walked it, the water levels rendered this impossible. Whichever route you take, you arrive at and follow the south side of the inlet. You go round the end of the inlet, bending right and following an excellent path, entering woodland. Near Hook Farm, about three quarters of a mile beyond the end of the inlet, you bend very sharp left and there is the luxury of an SBP sign! Pass Hook Farm, enjoying a super view to Hook House, heading just west of north to reach the signed Bewl Water Route. Turn right to follow a metalled road, and in just under half a mile you reach a kiosk, the main entrance to the complex. You may be asked your business, so don't be offended!

Turn right past the kiosk along a wide metalled road, keeping a waterworks to the left. The road soon bends sharp right, passing to the right of large wooden buildings, which are not marked on some maps. Just at the end of these buildings, turn left to bypass the gate which may be locked, then beyond the gate bear hard left and make your way down to the embankment path. It's now a lovely easy walk by Bewl Water, first along the embankment path then keeping woodland to the left. There's an obvious path throughout, hugging the water's edge including a big inlet, and after 2 miles or so from the start of the embankment path you reach a road. Turn right onto the road, crossing a bridge over the reservoir, then just beyond the bridge turn left along a clearly defined signed path. Initially it's a good green track, but it goes forward, as signed, to enter woodland heading south-east. Take care at a T-junction (not marked on maps) to turn right as signed, then continue through woods, going straight ahead at the path crossroads. Continue through and emerge from the woods, going forward to walk beside houses to arrive at the B2087 Flimwell-Ticehurst road at Union Street.

This next section is fiddly and difficult in places. Cross the road and turn left then immediately bear right along an initially clear path to reach the buildings of Quedley, with excellent views ahead. Beyond Quedley the path is less clear, kinking a little east of south. Follow the signposts, between holes of the Dale Hill golf course, taking care to walk to the right of the hedge, passing a GOLF IN PLAY sign. Keep walking to the right of the hedge, and take great care to turn right as signed across a fairway (be very careful of golfers and low-flying balls!), then bear left and enter the woods along a signed path. The path was almost submerged with dead leaves in places at the time of writing, and appeared to be not very well used or maintained. You rise to reach the edge of a field where a signpost points right and straight ahead. You take the "straight ahead" path but need to aim a little left of the way it points, downhill through the field, aiming for a gate and footbridge crossing as signed. Follow the footpath signposts beyond, your

A sign you are making progress round the edge of Sussex - a very Kentish sight near Wadhurst!

path going steeply uphill, and go round the left-hand edge of the Roughfield complex, walking along a narrow path in the woods, separated from the main driveway by a fence. You eventually join a driveway, the noise of the A21 now quite intrusive. As the buildings of Mumpumps are reached just short of the road, turn right as signed through a gate, then almost immediately left over a stile (this could be very easily missed) and then along the top of a back garden, arriving at the A21. Cross it with care, turn right, then opposite Mountpumps Oast bear left as signed. The way is clear to begin with, then at the hedge follow as signed to the right side of it, walking diagonally across to the right edge of this field, where you will see an SBP sign. Follow beside the right-hand field edge as signed, fractionally north of east, going forward to pass trees and keeping a stream to the right. Beyond the trees a very large field opens out to the left. Watch very carefully for and take a (very easily missed) signed path going away half-left, and bear left across the field to reach a track onto which you turn right, following it to Brookgate Farm. Turn right as you reach the complex, then almost immediately left as signed towards the house. The path looks private but isn't! Just before the house turn right then left along a track in the shade of trees, with a pond to the left. Look out very shortly for two footbridges off this track to the right, the left-hand one being the one you want. Cross it and beyond it go straight ahead as signed uphill through a field, woodland coming in from the right; walk along the right-hand field edge, keeping the woodland to the right. The path goes forward to become a track through the woods. Look carefully for a signed path going right just before the Delmonden Manor complex; take this path which goes eastwards, keeping an orchard to the right, crosses a track, and goes ahead very clearly through fields, to arrive at a road.

Turn left onto the road and immediately reach a road junction. Here turn hard right onto a signed very clear path through an orchard. Head south of east pretty much in a straight line (there is a very gentle right bend round to a T-junction where you turn left to continue, not marked on maps.) You negotiate a small area of trees as signed, then bear right, passing a sign warning of a bull in the field! Follow the right-hand field edge then very shortly bear left, eastwards, effectively following the field edge round. At the end, turn right then shortly left as signed, round the front of Rowland Farm, initially on a right-hand field edge; you then join a track which goes downhill then goes uphill and in due course becomes Hensill Lane, rising to reach a road. Turn right onto it then immediately left, almost at once reaching the A229 at the pretty village of The Moor, with a church directly opposite. It's likely a church has stood on this site since 1100, the chancel and north chapel being the oldest part of the existing church, most of which dates from around 1450. The great east window, built around 1350, is regarded as one of the finest pieces of architecture of its kind in the country.

The section ends here. You need to cross the A229 to continue, but by turning left and following the A229 for just over half a mile, you reach the centre of Hawkhurst with its excellent range of amenities.

SECTION 10 - **HAWKHURST (THE MOOR) - NORTHIAM**

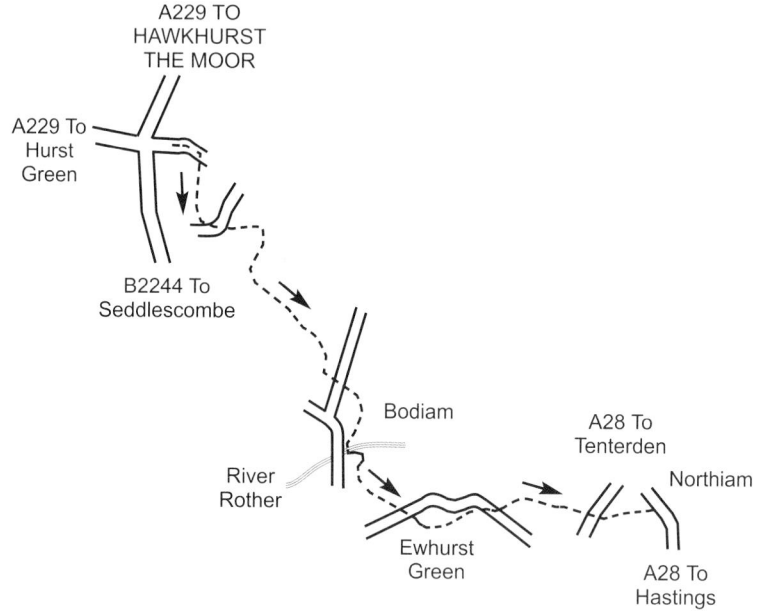

A229 TO
HAWKHURST
THE MOOR

A229 To
Hurst
Green

B2244 To
Seddlescombe

Bodiam

A28 To
Tenterden

Northiam

River
Rother

Ewhurst
Green

A28 To
Hastings

SECTION 10 - **HAWKHURST (THE MOOR) - NORTHIAM**

Length:	7 miles.
Public transport:	Regular buses serving Northiam on the Tenterden-Hastings route.
Refreshments:	Bodiam (P,C,S), Northiam (P,C,S).
Overview:	This is a very short section, deliberately so, because of three exceptional features close to or on the route which you may wish to take time out to enjoy: Bodiam Castle, the Kent & East Sussex Railway, and the Great Dixter gardens at Northiam. The scenery, particularly from Hawkhurst to Bodiam, is delightful and although 7 miles is not much walking for a single day, you may well end up spending the whole day on it!

Having crossed the A229, follow the road on the other side, keeping the church to the right, then at the crossroads at the end you cross the B2244 and enter Stream Lane. It soon bends left, then heads eastwards before veering right; shortly beyond the right bend, opposite Thainstone, take a signed footpath with the East Heath sign. Follow initially what is a very clear path south-eastwards past the East Heath buildings, then go forward downhill, the path becoming narrower. You pass an area of woodland which is to the left, then go forward uphill through a field, close to the right-hand field edge to reach a road, Conghurst Lane.

Turn left onto the road then almost immediately bear right along the Conghurst Farm road. Head eastwards through the farm complex, go on out the other side then start to descend, and three hundred yards or so beyond the farm turn right as signed, southwards, on a good path with splendid views. Cross a

Pointing the way between Hawkhurst and Bodiam

stream and continue on the path until the way forward is blocked by a fence and you need to turn sharp left, going uphill to the Northlands complex. Turn left just before the buildings and pass to the north side of them, soon reaching a footpath junction with SBP sign which has to be one of the most picturesquely sited SBP signs on the whole walk. Turn right at this junction onto a clear path south-eastwards, going downhill and through woods, then rise, still on a good path, to reach the buildings of Lower Northlands Farm. Go straight on as signed through the farm complex, going forward to follow a farm lane. This continues south-eastwards, veering southwards, then swings left, eastwards, to reach Bodiam Road.

Cross the road, turn right, then immediately bear left on a signed path uphill. Follow the direction indicated through the field then continue as signed across a track, aiming just to the left of the Court Lodge complex. From here you can now see Bodiam Castle. Bear right and follow the right-hand field edge downhill, the Court Lodge complex to your right and the castle straight ahead. You then follow a clear path just to the right of the field, dropping to reach a gate which you pass through to enter the Bodiam Castle grounds. Turn right to walk beside the moat, passing the bridge and keeping the moat to your left. At the corner bear left to continue beside the moat to its south-western corner, using the path from here to arrive at the useful shop and café. To continue, exit the castle complex just here and arrive at the road, but you will surely want to linger around the castle, arguably the finest castle in Sussex. It was built in 1385 as a response

Magnificent Bodiam Castle

The bridge over the Rother near Bodiam

to fears that the French might attempt an invasion via the nearby river Rother. It suffered severe damage in the English Civil War and fell into decay, but was restored at the end of the 19th century and a number of impressive features remain including gatehouse with portcullis, great hall, servants' hall, chapel and kitchen.
Turn left onto the road and follow it across the Rother by means of Bodiam Bridge. The SBP then turns left to follow the embankment by the Rother, but by continuing along the road you will soon reach the station at the western end of the preserved Kent & East Sussex Railway. The original railway ran from Robertsbridge to Headcorn via Tenterden, opening in the first decade of the 20th century; it closed to passengers in 1954 but twenty years later the section between Tenterden and Rolvenden was reopened as a preserved steam railway and the extension to Bodiam was effected in 2000. You may decide to indulge in a ride before continuing with the SBP! Back on the walking route, follow the right bank of the Rother eastwards of Bodiam Bridge. then just before the first gate, go right as signed and walk along the path to the railway. Turn right to shortly reach a gate crossing of the railway and cross here; turn left then immediately right to follow a signed path along a right-hand field edge. Continuing as signed just east of south, you go forward along a left-hand field edge, looking out for a path going off to the left, south-eastwards. Turn left to follow this path, which soon skirts the right-hand edge of some woodland; walk beside the woods, then bear left as signed past bushes, and shortly bear right as signed to follow a right-hand field edge uphill to reach the road

The crossing of the Kent and East Sussex Railway near Bodiam

at Ewhurst Green. Look back here for a stunning view of the Rother valley and Bodiam Castle.

Turn left to walk along the lovely main street at Ewhurst Green, going past the fine tile-hung Preacher's House and 12th century church to your right. Just beyond the church look out for and follow a signed path downhill (not SBP marked) along a left-hand field edge with an orchard immediately to your left. Soon you are directed into the orchard to continue, but keep on downhill in the same south-easterly direction, then at the bottom, turn left to follow the right-hand edge of the orchard north-eastwards. At the far north-eastern end, turn right to walk parallel with the road downhill, at length emerging onto the road and following it briefly. However, just before the bridge over the stream, turn left onto a path following the right-hand field edge, keeping the stream to your right. You cross the stream and enter another field, walking across it on an obvious path and aiming for another footbridge over the stream which describes an elaborate meander between footbridges! Don't cross this second footbridge (unless you wish to detour to visit Great Dixter - see below) but turn right onto a clear path, going south-eastwards and keeping the stream to your left. The path is well signed, continuing along a field close to its left edge, and a stream comes in to join you from the left. You cross it and immediately bear right to continue south-eastwards through another field, arriving at a road just by the house with the picturesque name Strawberry Hole.

Cross the road and immediately turn left just before the house along a signed path. It starts to climb, going forward to follow the left-hand field edge, and arrives at a gate, where you cross into another much bigger field which is cultivated. As you enter the field turn immediately right to follow its bottom end briefly, but almost at once bear left along a clear path uphill through the field. When you get level with modern houses that are to your left, look out for and take an unsigned path to the right, contouring the hill and aiming for the trees. At the very far corner of the field you join a little board walk through trees and then, on emerging, keep to the obvious signed path, which follows a right-hand field edge. You pass to the left of a house and go forward to join a wide gravelled lane, following it uphill to arrive at Northiam's main street. Cross the street and turn right to follow it, keeping the church to the left. The section ends here; there is a bus stop just beyond the church with a reasonable bus service to Rye and Hastings, and the village has a good range of refreshment opportunities. The showpiece of the village is an ancient battered oak on the green, held together by chains, and all round the green are weatherboarded 18th century houses while the church has a tall stone spire hidden behind a Norman base. Queen Elizabeth I dined at Northiam in 1573 and left some shoes which are kept at Brickwall, a large 17th century timber-framed house in the village. Northiam's greatest attraction is Great Dixter, a 15th century house with magnificent gardens which were designed by Edwin Lutyens and which include the Long Border with a spectacular mixture of shrubs and climbers.

SECTION 11 - **NORTHIAM - RYE**

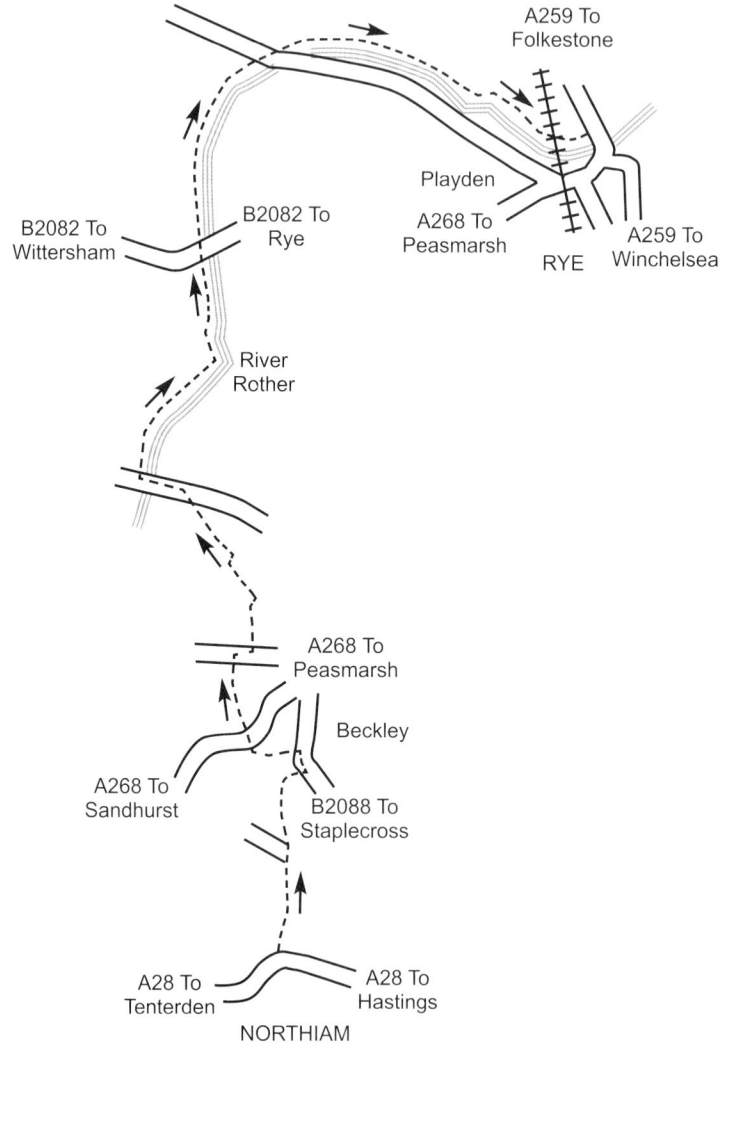

A259 To
Folkestone

Playden

B2082 To
Wittersham

B2082 To
Rye

A268 To
Peasmarsh

A259 To
Winchelsea

RYE

River
Rother

A268 To
Peasmarsh

Beckley

A268 To
Sandhurst

B2088 To
Staplecross

A28 To
Tenterden

A28 To
Hastings

NORTHIAM

SECTION 11 - **NORTHIAM - RYE**

Length:	10 miles.
Public Transport:	Regular trains serving Rye on the Brighton-Ashford International line.
Refreshments:	Rye (P,C,S).
Overview:	A fine conclusion to the "main" SBP with a splendidly straightforward and scenic finale along the banks of the Rother, culminating in one of the loveliest towns in Sussex. There is no convenient "split" but after a rather fiddly start the walking becomes very easy and there will be no problem concluding it in a day.

Having turned right onto Northiam's main street and passed the church which is on the left, you pass the sign for Hayes Inn which is also on the left, and you reach a little green. Take the driveway that cuts across the village green. As you approach 3 Acorn Cottage ahead, you need to turn hard left - at the time of writing there was a clear SBP sign here - up a drive which almost at once bends right and goes forward to a stile. Cross the stile and turn immediately left along the left-hand field edge path, going quite steeply downhill and skirting the right-hand edge of a wood. You're then signposted clearly on across the field beyond. At the end of this field you cross a narrow stream and veer very slightly left passing a small pool which is to your left, going over another field and straight on into a lovely wood with wild garlic in spring. You descend to cross a footbridge then climb to reach the far end of the wood. The map suggests you go straight on over the field but there's no path across it so you need to turn left and follow the left-hand field edge round until you see a signed path going away to the left.
Follow the clear path uphill, passing Woodgate House, and reaching a road. Turn left onto the road, almost immediately reaching a road junction. Turn right at this junction and follow the road briefly, then as it bends slightly right, turn left onto a signed path along a left-hand field edge, a large house immediately beside you to your left. You go forward into a large field with rough grass dotted about it, taking the direction of the arrow on the signpost, bringing you to stile just to the right of the very far top corner of the field. Turn right to cross the stile, then left to arrive at a field boundary and enter another large field. The map suggests you proceed diagonally across this field to a gate at the corner of the wood to your right, but the signage invites you to follow the left-hand field edge clockwise round to reach that point. From there, proceed along an obvious path south-eastwards to reach the B2088 at Beckley.

Turn left and follow the road briefly, then immediately past Beckley Village Centre, which is on your left, you turn left along a narrow but well-signed path through rough grass. Initially it's quite attractive with a stream to your left, but you then find yourself passing round a sewage works, veering right to pass to the north of the works and through an area of general farm/works debris, going forward along a clear path to reach the A268. Cross the road and turn right to follow beside the A268 for a few yards, soon reaching a large red-brick house which is to the right. Here you need to leave the road - the gate and signpost had been knocked down at the time of writing - and join the right-hand edge of the adjacent field to the left of the road. This shortly veers to the left, away from the road, and you follow it north-eastwards uphill along the right-hand field edge with woods to your right. Beyond the woods you reach a stile in the fence to the right. Cross the stile and keep on in the same north-easterly direction along what is a thin but still discernible path through a field, passing through a narrow strip of woodland and veering just north of east along the north fringe of Dean Wood. There is a stunning view from here along what is an excellent path, and there are seats provided for you to sit and enjoy the view. You drop down slightly to reach Hobbs Lane. Turn right to follow it briefly then as it veers to the right, you veer left onto a path along the left-hand field edge; the signage isn't good, perhaps explained by a couple of recently erected gates although if that is the explanation it's a shame the discs or finger posts haven't been restored! You arrive at an open field and here you need to bear right and follow the

The start of the Rother-side walk - now on the home stretch of the SBP!

Two swimmers on the Rother on the approach to Rye

right-hand field edge round to shortly enter another very pretty wood with an obvious path through it.

At the far end of the wood you cross a stile and arrive at a large field with a pond straight ahead. Aim just for the right of the pond and when you reach it you'll find a stile which you cross, aiming for a signpost with yellow strip painted on it. At that signpost you'll see a fork path junction. You need to take the left fork, going forward to follow a left-hand field edge, but as the boundary fence swings round to the right, take care to cross the stile and continue straight on in the same north-easterly direction, slightly downhill, to reach a double bridge. The first is an impressive modern wooden one, and having crossed that you turn immediately right, south-eastwards, to cross a tiny hump-back one and continue fleetingly in the same south-easterly direction. However you very shortly reach a fence going off to the left and a signed path going off to the left beyond the fence and parallel with it. It's signed High Weald Landscape Trail with which you're now overlapping. Walk north-eastwards parallel with the fence until it falls away to the left; don't fall away with it but carry on in the same direction, aiming for a stile just to the right of a large green barn (not marked on some maps) just ahead. Suddenly the ground falls away and you see and cross a nearer stile, going forward to the stile to the right of the barn, crossing that and going on in the same north-easterly direction; the path isn't too distinct but a signpost guides you. Initially you ascend, then begin to descend, still north-eastwards, proceeding downhill. You enter a small wood and go forward to reach a road onto which you turn left, shortly reaching the Blackwall Bridge crossing of the Rother.

Now the going gets very easy indeed and will remain so for the rest of the walk. You can give yourself a pat on the back - the hard fiddly walking is behind you! Having crossed the bridge turn immediately right to join a clear path along the left bank of the Rother, using the lower riverside path rather than the embankment. Simply follow this for 2 miles or so until you reach the B2082 Wittersham Road. You'll note a row of pylons coming in from the right, and some maps suggest that the bridlepath you're following, and the SBP with it, deviates briefly from the riverside at this point, but at the time of writing there was no signage to indicate this, and the crossing of a channel necessary to follow the "old" path was in very poor repair and could be dangerous. So stick to the riverside! Cross straight over the B2082 and continue eastwards then south-eastwards along the left bank of the Rother for just under 2 more miles. To your right across the river is the particularly fine set of hilltop buildings of Thornsdale Farm, with a splendid oast house, while ahead of you to the left is Stone Cliff, a prominent hillside just to the south of the historic village of Stone-in-Oxney.

In due course you reach the Military Road which you cross straight over. To your left is the Royal Military Canal, built in 1807 as a response to the threat of French invasion during the Napoleonic Wars; despite it being no more than 30ft wide it was capable of carrying both troops and equipment. Having crossed straight over the Military Road, turn right and then bear immediately left to continue beside the left bank of the Rother all the way to Rye, 3 miles distant. There is one point where you are signed round the left-hand side of a riverside house, and another where you need to drop down to pass under the railway - taller walkers need to mind their heads! - but otherwise it is straightforward walking although the Rother looks very muddy and unattractive just here. You're overlapping with the Saxon Shore Way and Royal Military Canal Path here on this concluding part of your walk; the Saxon Shore Way takes its name from a line of fortifications built along the coastline as it was in the 3rd century AD. At length, not long after passing under the railway, you reach the A259 coast road, which you last saw in Emsworth right at the start of the walk!

There seems to be some doubt from the maps and signs whether your arrival at the A259 marks the end of the SBP. Some maps suggest that it continues into the centre of Rye thus: turn right to follow the A259 over the Rother, continue to the junction with Fishmarket Road, turn right then immediately hard left into Landgate, going forward into Tower Street and then the A268 Cinque Ports Street, the station clearly visible down to the right via Station Approach. Much to be preferred is this: having crossed the Rother bridge, keep to the pavement on the left and veer away to the left with the Saxon Shore Way as signed to Rye Quay. Shortly you reach a children's playground immediately beyond which you turn right along a path which brings you back to the A259 Fishmarket. Cross straight over and climb the very steep steps which take you to East Cliff as it joins the High Street. Turn left and you're in the very centre of Rye. To reach the station, turn right along Market Road just beyond the Martello Bookshop, and walk downhill to reach Cinque Ports Street with Station Approach immediately opposite.

Rye is a wonderful place to finish your walk. This hilltop town, formerly a hill fort, became one of the Cinque Ports in the mid-14th century and was recognised as being of major strategic importance. The town's focal point is St Mary's Church which has a remarkable clock that is said to have the oldest functioning pendulum in England. Other features of interest are the 14th century Landgate, the 13th century Ypres Tower which was formerly a prison, the fine cobbled Mermaid Street with its splendid Mermaid Inn, the 17th century Old Grammar School in the High Street, the 15th century timber-framed Flushing Inn, the 18th century arcaded Town Hall, and the magnificent 18th century Lamb House in West Street where the novelists Henry James and later E.F. Benson lived. There are lots of cafes and pubs to celebrate your completion of the main walk.

That said, it's not quite over - if you want to say you've "done" the SBP, there's the little matter of the spur route roughly following the border between East and West Sussex...

The end of the SBP near Rye - not that you could tell from the signposting

SPUR SECTION 1 - **FISHERSGATE STATION - SCAYNES HILL**

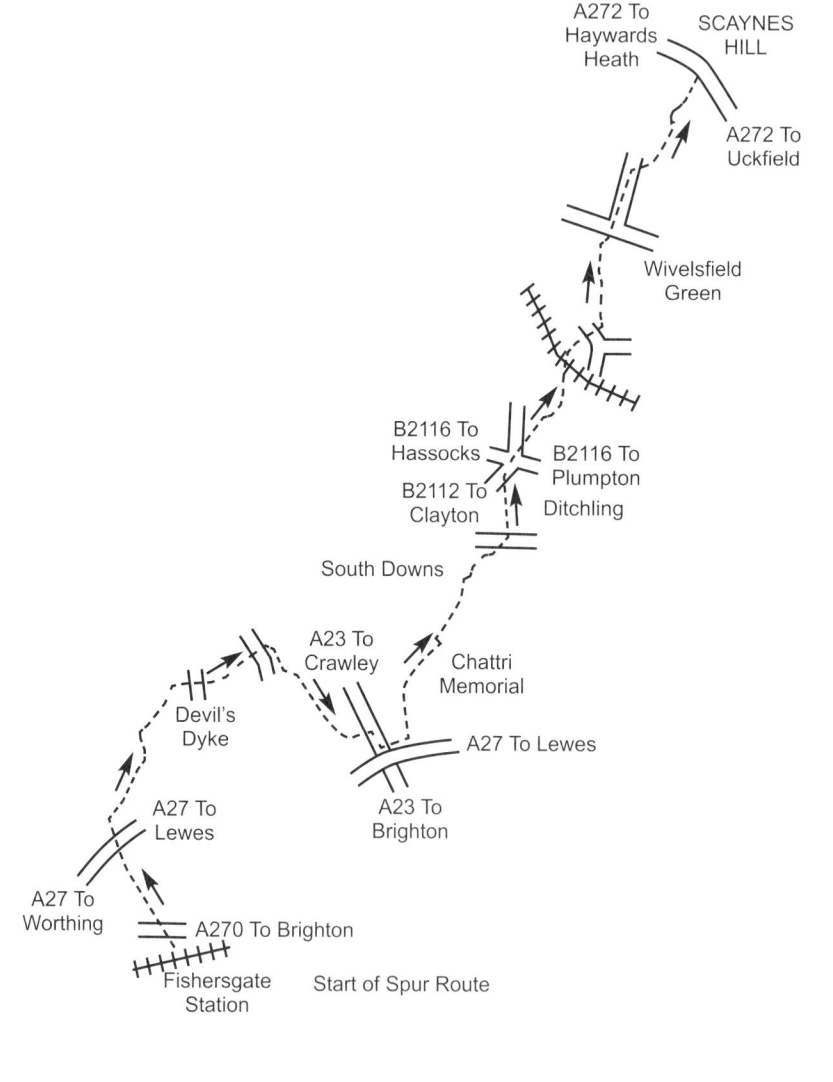

A272 To Haywards Heath

SCAYNES HILL

A272 To Uckfield

Wivelsfield Green

B2116 To Hassocks

B2116 To Plumpton

B2112 To Clayton

Ditchling

South Downs

A23 To Crawley

Chattri Memorial

A27 To Lewes

Devil's Dyke

A27 To Lewes

A23 To Brighton

A27 To Worthing

A270 To Brighton

Fishersgate Station

Start of Spur Route

SPUR SECTION 1 - FISHERSGATE STATION - SCAYNES HILL

Length:	14 miles.
Public Transport:	Regular trains serving Fishersgate on the Worthing-Brighton line; regular trains serving Hassocks on the London-Brighton line; regular buses serving Scaynes Hill on the Haywards Heath-Uckfield route.
Refreshments:	Devil's Dyke (P), Ditchling (P,C,S); Scaynes Hill (P,S).
Overview:	A superb walk climbing to and along the South Downs with spectacular views. Once beyond the lovely village of Ditchling (where the walk could easily be split), the walking is less obviously dramatic but still very enjoyable.

To begin the spur, exit Fishersgate station by the footpath heading north-westwards from the east end of the north platform, and walk north-westwards along a dead straight path, soon going over a road crossing and then shortly reaching the crossing of the A270 Old Shoreham Road. Continue straight over on the other side, still heading north-westwards and going uphill to another road crossing. It's at this point that according to the OS mapping the spur route officially starts, although at the time of writing there was no signage to confirm this. Go straight over and follow the path away from the road north-westwards; in a couple of hundred yards it bends sharply left and then right, keeping houses to your right and grass to your left. You arrive at a gate, immediately beyond which you need to veer left with the main path under two lines of pylons, then immediately having passed under the pylons veer slightly right to walk roughly parallel with the pylon lines. Ignore paths forking off left and right but continue along the obvious green path going forward, rising and arriving at a crossing of a rutted muddy track, with a gate close by to the left. Turn right onto the track which now goes downhill. A Monarch's Way disc is seen as you continue, passing beneath the pylons again and going over the top of the A27, veering left and continuing downhill north-westwards to arrive at a T-junction of paths. Turn right, almost immediately reaching another path junction, here turning hard left.

Follow what is a clear wide path uphill, initially northwards then north-eastwards uphill, veering right to arrive at another path T-junction. Turn left and walk just west of north uphill, soon passing a field boundary which is to the right, and another boundary a little further on on the left. Just over half a mile from the point at which you joined this path, there's a gate to the right, and you pass through this gate to follow a signed bridleway

The trig point at Sweet Hill between Devil's Dyke and Ditchling Beacon

heading off to the right and proceeding north-eastwards; the line is marked by a couple of wooden posts as the path is unclear through the field. Continue north-eastwards uphill, aiming for a gate in the next fence, and then keep plodding uphill in the same direction, aiming for the top of the scarp and the point where the fence ahead of you reaches the scarp top. Once you're on the top, turn right to join the South Downs Way, pausing for a moment to admire the superb views, then go forward to pass through a gate in the fence. Don't be tempted along the path following the north edge of the escarpment, but go straight on along a level grassy path, following the course of the South Downs Way, keeping a trig point to the left, and arrive at a road just to the right of the Devil's Dyke pub/restaurant. You may feel you've earned a rest and a drink here, but be warned, it is exceedingly popular in summer.

Go straight over the road and now follow the South Downs Way along a clear path going gently downhill north-eastwards, keeping the spectacular Devil's Dyke to your left. Legend has it that the cleft was created by the Devil who swore he would drown the churches of the Weald by cutting through the Downs thus letting in the sea, but he was frightened off by the crowing of cocks and left the job half done! Keep going along the South Downs Way, at length getting within sight of a car parking area and a road coming in from your right. Here you veer left with the South Downs Way, downhill, to arrive at a road at the hamlet of Saddlescombe. Turn left onto the road then very shortly right as signed with the South Downs Way, following the lane between houses and carrying on eastwards. You leave the houses behind and pass a bridleway leading off left, then carry on uphill through the trees to reach a path junction and gate. The South Downs Way then veers off to the left (north-east) but you fork off to the right, going through the gate (no SBP signage) and heading south-eastwards. The path is clear but can be extremely muddy. In roughly half a mile you reach a crossroads of paths where I found my first SBP marker on the spur route! Go straight over the crossroads and continue south-eastwards for another half mile or so, passing a footpath going hard off to the right and shortly beyond that, the triangulation point of Sweet Hill just to the right of the path, with good views to the West Blatchington windmill.

A short way beyond the triangulation point, there is a path junction where you need to turn left. All the way now till your return to the South Downs Way you need to observe the "Chattri and the Windmills" signposts; these may seem rather cryptic at first, but in due course you'll understand what's being referred to! Your path quickly curls to the right then heads north-eastwards, steeply downhill, and veers sharply to the right again. Don't continue along the clear track ahead but almost immediately turn left and then right as signed Chattri and the Windmills, going forward to a footbridge over the railway and A23. Bear left to cross the footbridge then on the other side turn right along a road which heads south-east to arrive close to the A27. Swing sharp left to walk parallel with the A27 along the road, passing a roundabout where there may be a refreshment van, although don't count on this!

The approach to the South Downs escarpment near Ditchling Beacon

Just beyond the roundabout you reach a junction with a road going off to the left, and immediately to the left of this latter road is a gate; go through the gate and join a path heading just west of north, uphill, keeping the last-mentioned road initially close by to your right. Ahead of you, to your half-right on the hillside, is a clump of trees and you can see the white Chattri Indian War Memorial. Unveiled in February 1921 by Edward Prince of Wales, it is dedicated to Indian soldiers who fought on the Western front during World War 1 and stands on the site where a number of them were cremated. At least you can now make sense of part of the "Chattri and the Windmills" sign! Your clear path heads northwards then equally clearly veers elegantly north-eastwards, passing above the trees and just to the left of the war memorial; the going remains very well defined and easy as you go forward past to the right of another area of trees and arrive at a path crossroads. Observing the Chattri and the Windmills sign, you go straight over the crossroads and carry on in the same direction, your path marked by a line of posts, rising to arrive at the South Downs Way again. This is as near as you'll get to the windmills referred to above, the Clayton (Jack and Jill) windmills, which can be accessed by turning left onto the South Downs Way at this point, and following it for just over half a mile. However the SBP spur turns right here to follow the South Downs Way eastwards, soon reaching a gate.

Pass through the gate and shortly you'll see, in the fence to the left, another gate with a signed bridleway beyond. There's no obvious path linking the South Downs Way with this gate, but don't let that worry you; simply cross the stony grass to the gate and go through it, following the direction shown by the bridleway arrow, heading north-eastwards. The path isn't terribly clear at first, but very shortly becomes much clearer as an often muddy path, marked on maps as Burnhouse Bostall. It heads down the hillside, veering to the right and then left, steeply descending all the time; do pause to enjoy the magnificent views across the Weald as you proceed downhill, as there is nothing quite as good as this to come. The gradient eases and it's then a straightforward descent to Underhill Lane.

Turn right onto Underhill Lane and shortly left onto a signed path which heads in a north/north-easterly direction between fences and which can be extremely squelchy. The signage is very clear as you pass stables and through a field where horses are kept. Pass through a gate and continue on just east of north along a right-hand field edge, veering a little west of north through a field as signed; there's no sign at the next field boundary but you now veer a little to the right to proceed to a footbridge over a stream, with housing to the right. Cross the footbridge and go forward to a mini-roundabout. Pass round the near side of the mini-roundabout and follow a narrow SBP signed path (there's also a No Cycling sign) which takes you to the top end of Beacon Road. Simply now go forward in the same direction beside the B2112 into the centre of Ditchling. The sometime home of the artist Sir Frank Brangwyn and the sculptor Eric Gill, and at the time of writing the home of the singer and "Forces' Sweetheart" Vera Lynn, Ditchling (formerly "Dicelinga," or settlement of the family or followers of a man called

Although the SBP isn't well signed in places, this is a welcome exception - near Scaynes Hill

Diccel) is a delightful village. It boasts a fine church with Norman and Early English features, and, over the road from the church, there's a Tudor house named Wing's Place with some excellent timberwork, while Eric Gill's calligraphy designs and woodcuts have been housed in the former village school. There's also a very nice café; although at the time of writing it had changed its name to the Ditchling Tea Rooms, previously it was known as Dolly's Pantry and did the most fantastic bacon and egg doorstep sandwiches. If you feel you've had enough for the day - and the sandwiches may just persuade you not to bother to exert yourself any further - you could easily break your journey at this point. Although buses may be infrequent, by heading west at the crossroads in the village centre along the B2116 you'll reach Hassocks in just a mile with excellent rail connections.

The SBP, however, continues northwards beyond the crossroads, shortly turning right into East Gardens. You veer immediately left and follow the lane, then just beyond a cream-coloured house on the left turn right as signed into a field, veering left to the field corner and going on into another field, aiming for the right-hand field boundary just short of the top corner. Cross into the adjacent field, bear left and go forward along a signed bridleway, soon passing through two tall gates. Continue just east of north to just short of a wooden slab where there's a bridleway sign pointing to the right, and here you need to bear right as signed, eastwards, following a lovely path through the woods. Veer sharp left, keeping to the obvious path and following it just east of north for nearly a mile, finally emerging at a field just short of the Burgess Hill-Lewes railway line. Veer half-left through the field to cross over the railway using the bridge, then turn hard right to walk parallel with the railway along the right-hand field edge, veering left at the field corner and continuing along the right-hand field edge as far as a footpath junction. Turn hard right, doubling back on yourself initially, then head just south of east to arrive at a road just south of a junction.

Turn left onto the road then immediately right at the junction onto a road heading east, but almost at once bear left along a signed bridleway; initially it's more of a lane, but beyond a footpath crossroads it narrows significantly. You reach another crossroads of paths where you need to turn left onto what is a clearly signed bridleway heading northwards through the edge of the woods, with fields visible to the left. This is certainly the most enjoyable walking since Ditchling and particularly pleasant and refreshing in hot sunshine. Occasionally there are paths going off it, but stick to the path that stays closest to the left (west) edge of the woods and you won't go wrong. After about a mile from the second path crossroads you emerge from the wood and continue to a T-junction with a road; turn right onto the road and follow it to a crossroads, now in Wivelsfield. There is a Wivelsfield railway station but this is in fact on the north edge of Burgess Hill, a good two and a half miles by road to the west, so don't be misled.

Go straight over into Slugwash Lane and follow it uphill to Towings Place, then continue along the road down to just before the Slugwash Kennels(in turn, just before a line of pylons) which are to the right. Just before the kennels turn right as signed along a path through the woods, which is well defined but could be muddy. Go over the obvious crossing track and continue north-eastwards to a river bridge known as Ham Bridge. The next quarter of a mile or so is tricky, so follow the directions given below carefully as the map will be of only limited assistance. Shortly beyond Ham Bridge you reach a gate; don't be tempted to veer right here with the lane but go straight on along a left-hand field edge to a stile and fingerpost. Bear left as signed then just before a footbridge turn right, again as signed, going over a wide farm track and along a clear path north-eastwards. Just beyond the next footbridge fork right onto a path which you follow steeply uphill, then go through a parking area and forward along a very narrow path to a T-junction with a metalled lane. Now things get a lot easier. Bear left onto the metalled lane and follow it all the way to a T-junction at the edge of the built-up area at the west end of Scaynes Hill. Bear right at the junction then immediately left along a straight path between houses, veering left just before the Farmers pub to reach the A272 in the centre of Scaynes Hill. This section ends here. The SBP crosses the road and turns right to pass the shop and garage then bears very shortly left along Clearwater Lane, but if you've walked all the way from Fishersgate you will deserve a night's rest.

Brooding skies on the South Downs en route for Ditchling

SPUR SECTION 2 - **SCAYNES HILL-EAST GRINSTEAD**

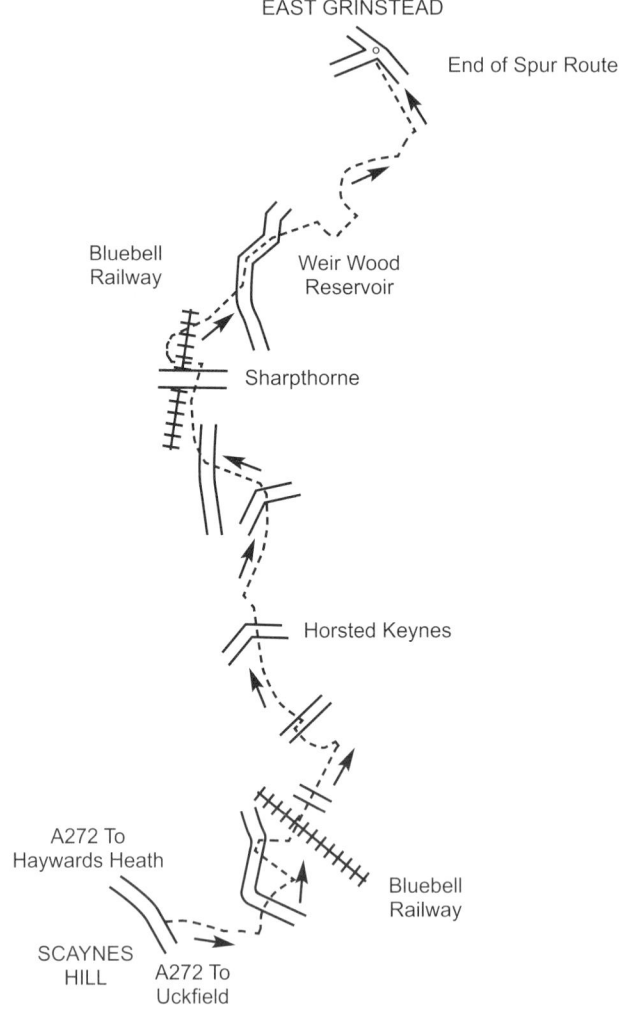

EAST GRINSTEAD

End of Spur Route

Bluebell Railway

Weir Wood Reservoir

Sharpthorne

Horsted Keynes

A272 To Haywards Heath

Bluebell Railway

SCAYNES HILL

A272 To Uckfield

SPUR SECTION 2 - **SCAYNES HILL - EAST GRINSTEAD**

Length:	12 miles.
Public transport:	East Grinstead - see section 6 above.
Refreshments:	Sloop (P); Horsted Keynes (P,S); Sharpthorne (P,S); East Grinstead (P,C,S).
Overview:	While lacking the drama of the previous spur section, this is a really enjoyable walk with a great variety of scenery including woodland and waterside walking and some fine panoramic views. Rail buffs will love the brush with the Bluebell Railway and the finale of the journey is a fine walk along part of the course of the now defunct East Grinstead-Groombridge line. Please note that while there are two sizeable villages on the route, there are no realistic public transport options which make it possible to break the journey.

Having turned left at Scaynes Hill into Clearwater Lane, follow the lane, initially fractionally north of east then just south of east, the lane petering out at the Hammond's Farm buildings. Go on round the right-hand edge of the buildings, swinging left then right, and continue eastwards, ignoring a misleading SBP sign pointing north; very soon, a correctly placed SBP finger post points you right, across the pasture, to another one pointing you left, downhill, with trees and a pond to your right. Keep walking downhill to a T-junction with a track, turning left here along the track to reach a footbridge and then continuing on in the same direction to a footpath T-junction. Bear left, uphill, keeping the fence to your right, but as you reach the crest of the hill, veer half-left, aiming just

Refreshment awaits between Scaynes Hill and Horsted Keynes

The impressive village church at Horsted Keynes

left of the prominent gate into the next field, and crossing a low stile. Follow the path as signed beyond the stile just east of north along the right-hand field edge, keeping immediately to the left of the trees and the buildings of Massetts, and arrive at a road, the picturesquely-named Butterbox Lane.

Turn right onto the road, pass the entrance to Massetts, and then shortly bear left up a driveway, soon forking right as signed along a path through the trees. Ascend gently and at the top of the rise, veer gently right to reach a path T-junction. For just a little while now you overlap with the Ouse Valley Way, a path which as the name suggests follows immediately beside or close to the course of the river Ouse, one of the major Sussex rivers; you'll see the river itself very soon. Bear left at the T-junction, dropping gently to enter woodland and follow a clear path through the wood, bearing left at a junction with a track, and following the track to the road. (You may note that this road has come from Scaynes Hill, following a considerably more direct course than the route you've just taken!) Turn right onto the road, and soon pass the Sloop pub, which must do well out of walkers, situated as it is on both the SBP and the Ouse Valley Way! You cross a bridge over the Ouse, then immediately beyond the bridge bear right as signed past the left-hand side of the buildings of Freshfield Mill Farm. Now follow the obvious signed path over stiles eastwards and go forward into a field, crossing a footbridge in the field and aiming for the south side of woodland. Follow the south fringe of the wood then swing left between two strips of woodland and pass under the Bluebell Railway. You will see plenty more of the Bluebell Railway later on but the section of line you can see here is part of the original preserved line between Sheffield Park and Horsted Keynes. Beyond the railway, follow a clear track uphill.

You could easily go wrong now, as the signage is particularly poor. When the woodland to the left of the track ends, don't continue along the track but aim half-right for the nearest bushes on the hilltop, veering north-eastwards; there's no path and no sign at this point, but aim for a signpost ahead, just to the left of the bushes, and the way suddenly becomes clear. Continue as signed beyond this signpost, and you'll see another post at the entry to King's Wood ahead. Follow the path through the wood, going over a crossing track to reach Ketche's Lane which you cross straight over, following a clear lane past Northland Farm. Beyond the farm, kink left then right as signed, through the woodland on a good path. The woodland gives way to a field to your left, and you continue almost to the top corner of the field where you reach a signed footpath junction. Take the path going hard left along a left-hand field edge then just before the field corner fork right along the left-hand field edge with trees to the left, descending to a metalled lane. Turn right onto the lane and, now heading just north of west, follow it all the way to Freshfield Lane.

Turn right into Freshfield Lane then shortly left into a field. Walk through the field as signed, going forward to reach a T-junction with a lane; turn right onto the lane and follow it, shortly veering sharp right and descending to just short of some gates. Here turn left as signed along an excellent path through woodland. Emerge and pass Wyatts, bearing left as signed but soon swinging right and following an obvious lane which veers left and crosses a crossroads to arrive at Horsted Keynes, just by the post office and a T-junction of roads.

Horsted Keynes has an attractive village green and refreshment opportunity in the form of a shop and pub, but it's best known for its station on the Bluebell Railway albeit this is some distance from the village centre. The preserved Bluebell Railway is part of the former line linking Lewes with East Grinstead, opening in 1882 and closing in 1955. It was forced to reopen a year later because the appropriate procedures had not

Lovely lake scenery between Horsted Keynes and Sharpthorne

been followed, and deliberately ran services at times of day which would have been no use to anybody. It finally closed for good in 1958, but two years later a preservation society was formed and the section between Sheffield Park and Horsted Keynes reopened. The preserved line has now been extended northwards to Kingscote just short of East Grinstead.

Back on the SBP, go straight over the T-junction in Horsted Keynes village centre onto a metalled lane, and go steeply downhill; you shortly meet a road coming from the left, and then ascend to the church. The church is mainly Norman in origin with a tall shingled spire, and one other feature of interest is a pigmy Crusader's effigy, which may have been scaled down to fit a niche in the chancel. Just short of the church, your road veers slightly left, passes to the left of the church and continues on to a gate; go through the gap to the right of the gate and forward along a really lovely path which passes between large ponds. Seats are provided, and you may well be tempted to sit and relax and enjoy the tranquillity. You reach a fork junction where you're signed left, soon veering round to the right within sight of the fine Broadhurst Manor, mostly built in 1934 but with some 16th century features; bear left here and walk up to a T-junction with Hurstwood Lane.

Turn left onto Hurstwood Lane and soon arrive at another T-junction, bearing right to follow this road. Look out shortly for a thatched building to the left, and just before it bear left as signed, following a right-hand field edge north-westwards downhill then

The Bluebell Railway near Sharpthorne

round to the left. Bear right as signed downhill to a footbridge then steeply uphill and along a right-hand field edge. Again bear round to the left, and again bear right into woodland, and again go downhill. This time though you bear left and then right as signed over a narrow footbridge, veering left up through a field to Horsted Lane. Bear right then left at a sign for Northwood House, going downhill then shortly right along a signed path. The next piece of walking is fiddly so take care, ensuring you observe the signposts. Follow the left-hand field edge, going forward as signed, just west of north over a field to a track. Cross straight over it and go north-westwards over the next field, keeping a modern building well to the left, and now veer just east of north to go downhill as signed through a wider field to the corner of a wood. Cross two stiles, bearing left, to walk uphill along a left-hand field edge,

A rustic footbridge on the approach to Sharpthorne

bearing right just before the next boundary, turning left again to cross a stile and then going forward along a right-hand field edge enjoying glorious views. Go forward into a wood along a narrow path, just at the end bearing left and then right to reach Sharpthorne's main street, Top Road. Sharpthorne is an unremarkable village but does provide some refreshment opportunity; at the time of writing the village store offered takeaway hot drinks as well as cold snacks, and as East Grinstead is still some way ahead, you are strongly advised to take advantage!

Bear right onto Top Road, then first left into Station Road. Veer round to the left over the railway, then veer right to walk parallel with the Bluebell Railway downhill. If trains are running you can enjoy the sight and sound of the magnificent old steam engines. The road becomes a signed public footpath, actually a narrow lane, which you continue to follow, avoiding the temptation to go over the "level" railway crossing. The lane goes round to the right, under the railway, and you continue along it north-eastwards, keeping the New Coombe Farm to the right. Go forward along the lane which becomes a narrow path through a field and enters a wood; having entered the wood, turn left as signed, then veer right, ignoring a left fork, and go on uphill, across a wide track, following an obvious path to Grinstead Lane. Turn left onto this lane, cross the end of Weir Wood Reservoir, and carry on north-eastwards uphill along the lane.

The Weir Wood Reservoir between Sharpthorne and East Grinstead

A tree shaded path near the Weir Wood Reservoir

As the lane swings left, turn right onto a road (effectively first right beyond the reservoir crossing) and follow the road which heads for the reservoir. It peters out but continue along a signed path, which snakes along the reservoir edge, keeping it to the right albeit sometimes separated by vegetation. Ignore two signed paths going off to the left and pass through some lovely woodland; with the twists and turns this waterside walk may take quite a lot longer than one perhaps thinks it should. Not far before the east end of the reservoir you pass a picnic area and a little way beyond that, you'll see an SBP sign pointing you to the left. Turn left here along an obvious path to Busses Farm; pass just to the left of the farm buildings then go round to the right, keeping a pond to the left. Having veered right by the pond, you reach a junction with a byway signed straight on, and an SBP signed fork to the right. In obedience to the SBP sign, fork right to enter the meadow and follow it downhill, north-eastwards, to walk along the left-hand edge of the fields with woodland to the left. The path isn't too well defined and there's no signage, so you may wonder if you're correct, and with the end so close now, this would be a particularly ironic time to lose the route! You go through a gate, again with no SBP sign, and veering in a more easterly direction, you go forward through a larger field to a footbridge. Cross over it and go forward to a T-junction with a lane, with a sewage works to the left. Turn left here to follow the lane to a bridge over the Forest Way, bearing right just before the bridge along a slipway to reach the Forest Way. Now all your route-finding troubles are over and you can enjoy a grandstand finish to your walk as you turn

The final stretch of the spur route near East Grinstead

hard left to walk along the Forest Way; this is part of the course of the old railway line linking East Grinstead with Groombridge, which you will have seen further east on the Ashurst-Wadhurst section of the main SBP. Simply follow the Forest Way in a dead straight line north-westwards into the outskirts of East Grinstead. As you enter the built-up area you cross a road and go uphill, reaching a path fork; take the left fork here, and go forward to reach what is the end of East Grinstead's main street. Bear left and pass Sackville College to enter East Grinstead and end the spur. To access the station, turn right in the centre of the town onto London Road and then left into Railway Approach, soon reaching a roundabout beyond which is Sainsbury's and the station itself. Congratulations - you have completed the whole of the Sussex Border Path and you will certainly have deserved your celebratory meal or drink in one of the many cafes or restaurants the town has to offer.

A delightful and straightforward stretch of field edge walking on the second half of the SBP spur route

Contrasting pathways on the SBP spur route